Invasive Exotic Plant Monitoring at Wilson's Creek National Battlefield: Year 1 (2006)

Natural Resource Technical Report NPS/HTLN/NRTR—2007/013
NPS D-76

Craig C. Young, Jennifer L. Haack, and Holly J. Etheridge
National Park Service, Heartland I&M Network
Wilson's Creek National Battlefield, 6424 West Farm Road 182, Republic, MO 65738

Heartland
Network
Natural Resource Monitoring

March 2007

U.S. Department of the Interior
National Park Service
Natural Resource Program Center
Fort Collins, Colorado

The Natural Resource Publication series addresses natural resource topics that are of interest and applicability to a broad readership in the National Park Service and to others in the management of natural resources, including the scientific community, the public, and the NPS conservation and environmental constituencies. Manuscripts are peer-reviewed to ensure that the information is scientifically credible, technically accurate, appropriately written for the intended audience, and is designed and published in a professional manner.

The Natural Resource Technical Report series is used to disseminate the peer-reviewed results of scientific studies in the physical, biological, and social sciences for both the advancement of science and the achievement of the National Park Service's mission. The reports provide contributors with a forum for displaying comprehensive data that are often deleted from journals because of page limitations. Current examples of such reports include the results of research that addresses natural resource management issues; natural resource inventory and monitoring activities; resource assessment reports; scientific literature reviews; and peer reviewed proceedings of technical workshops, conferences, or symposia.

Views and conclusions in this report are those of the authors and do not necessarily reflect policies of the National Park Service. Mention of trade names or commercial products does not constitute endorsement or recommendation for use by the National Park Service.

Printed copies of reports in these series may be produced in a limited quantity and they are only available as long as the supply lasts. This report is also available from the Heartland I&M Network website (http://www.nature.nps.gov/im/units/HTLN) on the internet, or by sending a request to the address on the back cover.

Please cite this publication as:

Young, C.C., J.L. Haack, and H.J. Etheridge. 2007. Invasive exotic plant monitoring at Wilson's Creek National Battlefield: Year 1 (2006). Natural Resource Technical Report NPS/HTLN/NRTR—2007/013 National Park Service, Fort Collins, Colorado.

NPS D-76, March 2007

Acknowledgements

Dan Tenaglia conducted all field work associated with this report in 2006. Dan was killed on February 13, 2007 following a collision two days earlier while riding his bike near his home in Opelika, Alabama. We are grateful for his work. Dan's botanical photography can be found at his Missouri Plants website: http://www.missouriplants.com/.

Executive Summary

During surveys in 2006, we documented 35 invasive, exotic plant species on Wilson's Creek National Battlefield. Eleven of these exotic plant species were not previously documented as occurring on the park based on NPSpecies, the service-wide database for plant information. Sericea lespedeza, the most abundant invasive plant at Wilson's Creek National Battlefield, covered between 480 and 851 acres. The plant most likely spread into restored grasslands from areas where it was planted. While we believe that the cover was overestimated, the plant is clearly widespread and abundant on the park. Two species, crownvetch and autumn olive, with high ecological impacts were noted as having low management difficulty. Of the 35 invasive plant species, 26 species occurred in less than 18 % of transects and covered less than 1 acre. The relatively low cover of these species is encouraging and suggests that eradication or at least successful control may be a viable management option. In general, several exotic plants are a major problem at Wilson's Creek National Battlefield, but successful control is possible for a large group of species. The acreage estimates presented in the report may be used to plan management activities leading to control of exotic plants and the accomplishment of GPRA goal IA1b.

Table of Contents

This page intentionally left blank.

Introduction

Author's note. In this report, we use the term invasive exotic plant to refer to plants that are not native to the park and that are presumed to pose environmental harm to native plant populations and/or communities based on a review of numerous state and regional invasive exotic plant lists. The great majority of the introductory text was taken from Welch and Geissler (2007) with slight modification.

Scope of invasive exotic plant problem for National Parks. Globalization of commerce, transportation, human migration, and recreation in recent history has introduced invasive exotic species to new areas at an unprecedented rate. Biogeographical barriers that once restricted the location and expansion of species have been circumvented, culminating in the homogenization of the Earth's biota. Although only 10% of introduced species become established and only 1% become problematic (Williamson 1993, Williamson and Fitter 1996) or invasive, nonnative species have profound impacts worldwide on the environment, economies, and human health. Invasive species have been directly linked to the replacement of dominant native species (Tilman 1999), the loss of rare species (King 1985), changes in ecosystem structure, alteration of nutrient cycles and soil chemistry (Ehrenfeld 2003), shifts in community productivity (Vitousek 1990), reduced agricultural productivity, and changes in water availability (D'Antonio and Mahall 1991). Often the damage caused by these species to natural resources is irreparable and our understanding of the consequences incomplete. Invasive species are second only to habitat destruction as a threat to wildland biodiversity (Wilcove et al. 1998). Consequently, the dynamic relationships among plants, animals, soil, and water established over many thousands of years are at risk of being destroyed in a relatively brief period.

For the National Park Service (NPS), the consequences of these invasions present a significant challenge to the management of the agency's natural resources "unimpaired for the enjoyment of future generations." National Parks, like other land management organizations, are deluged by new exotic species arriving through predictable (e.g., road, trail, and riparian corridors), sudden (e.g., long-distance dispersal through cargo containers and air freight), and unexpected anthropogenic pathways (e.g., weed seeds in restoration planting mixes). Nonnative plants claim an estimated 4,600 acres of public lands each year in the United States (Asher and Harmon 1995), significantly altering local flora. For example, exotic plants comprise an estimated 43% and 36% of the flora of the states of Hawaii and New York, respectively (Rejmanek and Randall 1994). Invasive plants infest an estimated 2.6 million acres of the 83 million acres managed by the NPS.

More NPS lands are infested daily despite diligent efforts to curtail the problem. Impacts from invasive species have been realized in most parks, resulting in an expressed need to control existing infestations and restore affected ecosystems. Additionally, there is a growing urgency to be proactive—to protect resources not yet impacted by current and future invasive species (Marler 1998). Invasive exotic species most certainly will continue to be a management priority for the National Parks well into the 21st Century. Invasive exotic plants have been consistently ranked as a top vital sign for long term monitoring as part of the NPS Inventory & Monitoring (I&M) Program. During the vital signs selection process in 2003, Heartland Network parks recognized the need for exotic plant monitoring (DeBacker et al. 2004). Nine parks (CUVA, EFMO, GWCA, HEHO, HOCU, HOME, LIBO, OZAR, PERI) identified invasive exotic plants as their most important management issue, two parks (TAPR, WICR) identified invasive exotic plants as their second most important management issue, and PIPE identified invasive exotic plants as its third most important management issue. During this process, invasive exotic plant monitoring was recognized across all network parks as the most important shared monitoring need.

Prevention and early detection as keys to invasive exotic plant management. Prevention and early detection are the principal strategies for successful invasive exotic plant management. While there is a need for long-term suppression programs to address very high-impact species, eradication efforts are most successful for infestations less than one hectare in size (Rejmanek and Pitcairn 2002). Eradication of infestations larger than 100 hectares is largely unsuccessful, costly, and unsustainable (Rejmanek and Pitcairn 2002). Costs, or impacts, to ecosystem components and processes resulting from invasion also increase dramatically over time, making ecosystem restoration improbable in the later stages of invasion. Further, in their detailed review of the nonnative species problem in the United States, the US Congress, Office of Technology Assessment (1993) stated that the environmental and economic benefits of supporting prevention and early detection initiatives significantly outweigh any incurred costs, with the median benefit-to-cost ratio being 17:1 in favor of being proactive.

Although preventing the introduction of invasive exotic plants is the most successful and preferred strategy for resource managers, the realities of globalization, tight fiscal constraints, and limited staff time guarantee that invaders will get through park borders. Fortunately, invasive exotic plants quite often undergo a lag period between introduction and subsequent colonization of new areas. Managers, then, can take advantage of early detection monitoring to make certain invasive exotic species are found and successfully eradicated before populations become well established.

This strategy requires resource managers to: (1) detect invasive exotic species early (i.e., find a new species or an incipient population of an existing species while the infestation is small (less than 1 hectare), and (2) respond rapidly (i.e., implement appropriate management techniques to eliminate the invasive plant and all of its associated regenerative material).

Invasive exotic plant management at Wilson's Creek National Battlefield. Invasive exotic plant management is a high management priority at Wilson's Creek National Battlefield. While a complete history of park invasive exotic plant management issues is beyond the scope of this report, a few important highlights are given:

1. Invasive exotic plants, such as annual brome (*Bromus* spp.), hop clover (*Trifolium campestre*), and sericea lespedeza (*Lespedeza cuneata*) occur in glades supporting the federally endangered Missouri bladderpod (*Lesquerella filiformis*).

2. Invasive plants, such as Kentucky bluegrass (*Poa paretensis*) and sericea lespedeza, have invaded restored native warm season grasslands.

3. Early successional forests at the park support numerous invasive exotic plant species.

Methods

Watch lists. The invasive exotic plants on three watch lists were sought during monitoring (Table 1). Invasive exotic plants not known to occur on the park based on NPSpecies (the national NPS database for plant occurrence registration) constitute the early detection watch list. Invasive exotic plants known to occur on the park based on NPSpecies constitute the park-established watch list. Invasive exotic plants from the park-based watch list included plants selected by park managers or network staff which may not have been included on the other lists due to incomplete information in NPSpecies (e.g., not documented) or USDA Plants (e.g., state distribution information inaccurate) databases or due to differing opinions regarding network designation of a plant as a high priority. While aquatic species are listed on the watch lists, terrestrial plants were the focus of this survey. Aquatic plants were documented occasionally.

Field methods. Invasive exotic plant species on designated watch lists (Table 1) were sought in high priority areas on Wilson's Creek National Battlefield (Figure 1). Dan Tenaglia, the contract botanist for this project, used a Thales GPS unit to navigate along 200 m line transects, identified invasive exotic plants in an approximately 6-m belt, and attributed a coarse cover value to each species ($0=0$, $1=0.1-0.9$ m^2, $2=1-9.9$ m^2, $3=10-49.9$ m^2, $4=50-99.9$ m^2, $5=100-499.9$ m^2, $6=499.9-999.9$ m^2, $7=1000-4999.9$ m^2, $8=5000-9999.9$ m^2, and $9=10,000-14999.9$ m^2). A total of 173 transects were surveyed at Wilson's Creek National Battlefield. Of these, 100 transects were 200 m in length, while 40 were 0-99 m in length and 31 were 100-199 m in length. The observer had discretion to search a larger belt if feasible, to search additional areas up to 100 m perpendicular distance from the transect, to target locations likely to support exotic plants (e.g., field edges, roads), and to circumvent extremely difficult or hazardous terrain when needed. However, in most cases, the observer maintained the established line transect. Cover was estimated for all plants observed while navigating along the transect (i.e., not restricted to the 6-m belt).

Analytical methods. Data analysis involved simple displays, as well as calculation of plant frequency and cover. The invasive exotic plants encountered on Wilson's Creek National Battlefield were attributed to line transects in a GIS. Polygons surrounding occupied line transects were highlighted on maps for each invasive exotic plant encountered (Figures 2 – 36). Note that entire polygons were not fully searched. The park-wide frequency of invasive exotic plants was calculated as the percentage of occupied transects. A park-wide cover range was estimated using the high and low values of the cover classes for each invasive exotic plant encountered, assuming that 6 % of the park was searched and that the areas searched were representative of the entire park.

Invasiveness ranks. In order to provide additional information on the ecological impact and feasibility of control, the ecological impact and general management difficulty sub-ranks that constitute the invasiveness rank (I-rank), as determined by NatureServe (Morse et al. 2004), were listed when available. The ecological impact characterizes the effect of the plant on ecosystem process, community composition and structure, native plant and animal populations, and the conservation significance of threatened biodiversity. General management difficulty ranks are assigned based on the resources and time generally required to control a plant, the non-target effects of control on native populations, and the accessibility of invaded sites. Sub-ranks are given as high (H), medium (M), low (L), insignificant (I), unknown (U), or a combination of ranks.

Results and Discussion

In 2006, a total of 35 invasive exotic plant taxa were found during the survey at Wilson's Creek National Battlefield (Table 2). Of these plants, 22 taxa were known to occur on the park based on the NPSpecies database. Bald brome (*Bromus racemosus*) was not previously included on any watch list. Bald brome is not designated as a high priority for the entire network, but is wide-spread at WICR. These species will be added to the park-based watch list. The species on the early detection list will be entered in NPSpecies and should subsequently be included on the park-established watch list.

The distribution and abundance of the invasive exotic plant species at Wilson's Creek National Battlefield varied widely. Four species were widespread and very abundant (cover greater than 60 acres): bald brome, sericea lespedeza (*Lespedeza cuneata*), Japanese honeysuckle (*Lonicera japonica*), and Osage orange (*Maclura pomifera*). Smooth brome (*Bromus inermis*) was also very abundant, but restricted to a single section of the park. Fescue (*Schedonorus* spp.), smooth sumac (*Rhus glabra*), multiflora rose (*Rosa multiflora*), and hegdeparsley (*Torilis* spp.) were moderately abundant (cover 2 – 25 acres) and distributed widely on the park. Amur honeysuckle (*Lonicera maackii*) was moderately abundant, but restricted to a few locations on the park. The remaining 26 species occurred in less than 18 % of transects and covered less than 1 acre. The relatively low cover of these species is encouraging and suggests that eradication or at least successful control is likely to be a viable management option.

Based on field observations, we believe that the cover of invasive exotic plant species, especially those with high cover estimates, were systematically overestimated. Such overestimation likely resulted from difficulty estimating high cover over the 200 m transects. While such overestimation may complicate detection of change in the future, the relative size of cover estimates provides a strong basis for invasive exotic plant management planning.

Three species were noted as having unambiguously high ecological impact: cheatgrass (*Bromus tectorum*), crownvetch (*Securigera varia*), and autumn olive (*Elaeagnus umbellata*) (Table 2). Five species were characterized as having at least a medium ecological impact. The remaining species had ambiguous medium-low ecological impacts or less, including three species with low or insignificant impacts. Recognizing that the feasibility of control often strongly influences decisions regarding invasive exotic plant management, crownvetch and autumn olive with high ecological impacts were noted as having low management difficulty. Controlling these species will likely provide a high benefit for the management costs.

In summary, this report provides information on invasive exotic plant abundance and distribution as well as ecological impacts and management difficulty to assist park natural resource managers in planning invasive exotic plant management. The following links may further assist managers: http://www.nature.nps.gov/im/units/htln/monitoring/projects/inp.htm and http://www.natureserve.org/explorer/.

Literature Cited

Asher, J. A., and D. W. Harmon. 1995. Invasive exotic plants are destroying the naturalness of U.S. Wilderness areas. International Journal of Wilderness 1:35-37.

D'Antonio, C. M., and B. E. Mahall. 1991. Root profiles and competition between the invasive, exotic perennial, *Carpobrotus edulis,* and two native shrub species in California coastal scrub. American Journal of Botany 78:885-894.

DeBacker, M.D., C.C. Young (editor), P. Adams, L. Morrison, D. Peitz, G.A. Rowell, M. Williams, and D. Bowles. 2005. Heartland Inventory and Monitoring Network and Prairie Cluster Prototype Monitoring Program Vital Signs Monitoring Plan. National Park Service, Heartland Inventory and Monitoring Network and Prairie Cluster Prototype Monitoring Program, Wilson's Creek National Battlefield, Republic, Missouri, 104 pp. plus appendices.

Ehrenfeld, J.G. 2003. The effects of exotic plant invasions on soil nutrient cycling processes. Ecosystems 6:503-523.

King, W. B. 1985. Island birds: will the future repeat the past? Pages 3-15 *in* P. J. Moors, editor. Conservation of Island Birds. International Council for Bird Preservation. Cambridge University Press, Cambridge, UK.

Marler, M. 1998. Exotic plant invasions of federal Wilderness areas: current status and future directions. The Aldo Leopold Wilderness Research Institute. Rocky Mountain Research Station, Missoula, Montana, USA.

Office of Technology Assessment. 1993. Harmful non-indigenous species in the United States. OTA-F-565. U.S. Congress, Government Printing Office, Washington, D.C., USA.

Rejmanek, M., and M. J. Pitcairn. 2002. When is eradication of exotic pest plants a realistic goal? Pages 249-253 in C. R. Veitch and M. N. Clout, editors. Turning the Tide: the Eradication of Invasive Species. IUCN SSC Invasive Species Specialist Group. IUCN, Gland, Switzerland and Cambridge, UK.

Rejmanek, M., and J. M. Randall. 1994. Invasive alien plants in California: 1993 summary and comparison with other areas in North America. Madrono 41:161–177.

Tilman, D. 1999. The ecological consequences of changes in biodiversity: a search for general principles. Ecology 80:1455-1474.

Vitousek, P. M. 1990. Biological invasions and ecosystem processes: towards an integration of population biology and ecosystem studies. Oikos 57:7-13.

Welch, B.A. and P.H. Geissler. 2007. Early detection of invasive plants: a handbook. United States Geological Survey draft. http://www.pwrc.usgs.gov/brd/invasiveHandbook.cfm.

Wilcove, D. S., D. Rothstein, J. Dubow, A. Phillips, and E. Losos. 1998. Quantifying threats to imperiled species in the United States. Bioscience 48:607–615.

Williamson, M. 1993. Invaders, weeds and risk from genetically modified organisms. Experientia 49:219–224.

Williamson, M. and A. Fitter. 1996. The varying success of invaders. Ecology 77:1661–1666.

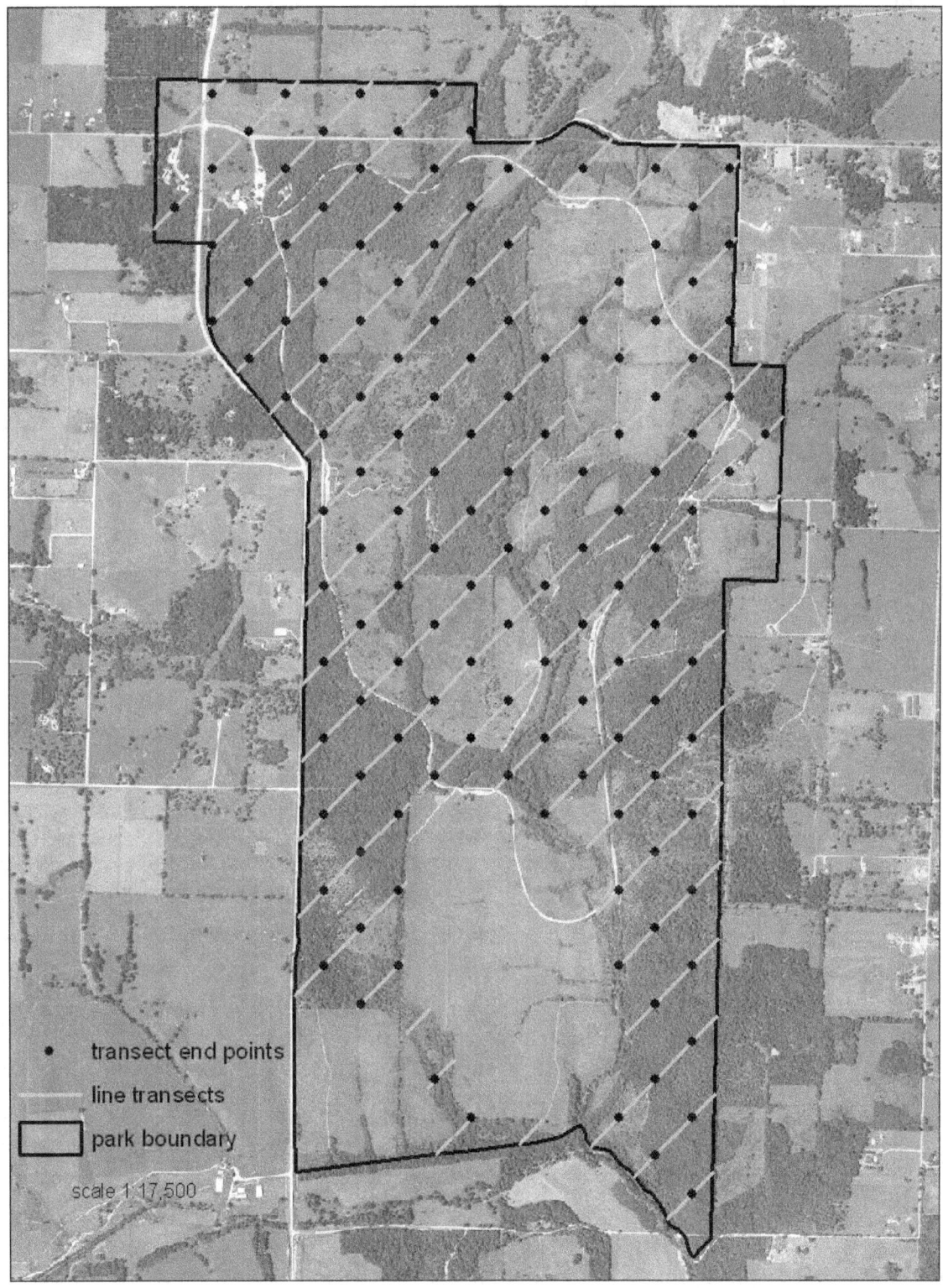

Figure 1. Invasive exotic plant line transects (blue) at Wilson's Creek National Battlefield. The blue transects indicate the search locations for invasive exotic plants in 2006.

Table 1. Watch lists for Wilson's Creek National Battlefield.

Early Detection Watch List		Park-Established Watch List		Park-Based Watch List	
Acer ginnala	Amur maple	*Arctium minus*	Lesser burdock	*Bromus racemosus*	Bald brome
Ailanthus altissima	Tree-of-heaven	*Bromus inermis*	Smooth brome	*Ligustrum vulgare*	Common privet
Albizia julibrissin	Silktree	*Bromus sterilis*	Poverty brome	*Lolium perenne*	Perennial ryegrass
Alliaria petiolata	Garlic mustard	*Bromus tectorum*	Cheatgrass	*Vicia villosa*	Winter vetch
Alnus glutinosa	European alder	*Carduus nutans*	Nodding plumeless thistle		
Arundo donax	Giant reed	*Dactylis glomerata*	Orchardgrass		
Azolla spp.	Mosquitofern	*Dipsacus fullonum*	Fuller's teasel		
Berberis thunbergii	Japanese barberry	*Hedera helix*	English ivy		
Bothriochloa bladhii	Caucasian bluestem	*Hesperis matronalis*	Dames rocket		
Celastrus orbiculatus	Oriental bittersweet	*Holcus lanatus*	Common velvetgrass		
Centaurea stoebe ssp. *micranthos*	Spotted knapweed	*Humulus japonicus*	Japanese hop		
Centaurea solstitialis	Yellow star-thistle	*Lespedeza cuneata*	Sericea lespedeza		
Cirsium arvense	Canada thistle	*Lonicera japonica*	Japanese honeysuckle		
Cirsium vulgare	Bull thistle	*Maclura pomifera*	Osage orange		
Cornus foemina	Stiff dogwood	*Melilotus officinalis*	Sweetclover		
Cynanchum louiseae	Black swallowwort	*Morus alba*	White mulberry		
Cynanchum rossicum	European swallowwort	*Phalaris arundinacea*	Reed canarygrass		
Dioscorea oppositifolia	Chinese yam	*Plantago lanceolata*	Narrowleaf plantain		
Dipsacus laciniatus	Cutleaf teasel	*Poa compressa*	Canada bluegrass		
Egeria densa	Brazilian waterweed	*Poa pratensis*	Kentucky bluegrass		
Eichhornia crassipes	Common water hyacinth	*Potentilla recta*	Sulphur cinquefoil		
Elaeagnus angustifolia	Russian olive	*Rhus glabra*	Smooth sumac		
Elaeagnus umbellata	Autumn olive	*Robinia pseudoacacia*	Black locust		
Euonymus alata	Burningbush	*Rosa multiflora*	Multiflora rose		
Euonymus fortunei	Winter creeper	*Schedonorus phoenix*	Tall fescue		
Euphorbia esula	Leafy spurge	*Schedonorus pratensis*	Meadow fescue		
Glechoma hederacea	Ground ivy	*Sorghum halepense*	Johnsongrass		
Lespedeza bicolor	Shrub lespedeza	*Torilis arvensis*	Spreading hedgeparsley		
Ligustrum sinense	Chinese privet	*Torilis japonica*	Erect hedgeparsley		

Table 1. Watch lists for Wilson's Creek National Battlefield (cont.)

Early Detection Watch List		Park-Established Watch List		Park-Based Watch List
Lonicera maackii	Amur honeysuckle	*Ulmus pumila*	Siberian elm	
Lonicera morrowii	Morrow's honeysuckle	*Verbascum thapsus*	Common mullein	
Lotus corniculatus	Bird's-foot trefoil			
Lysimachia nummularia	Creeping jenny			
Lythrum salicaria	Purple loosestrife			
Melia azedarach	Chinaberrytree			
Microstegium vimineum	Nepalese browntop			
Miscanthus sinensis	Chinese silvergrass			
Myriophyllum aquaticum	Parrot feather watermilfoil			
Myriophyllum spicatum	Eurasian watermilfoil			
Pastinaca sativa	Wild parsnip			
Paulownia tomentosa	Princesstree			
Phragmites australis	Common reed			
Polygonum cuspidatum	Japanese knotweed			
Populus alba	White poplar			
Populus tremuloides	Quaking aspen			
Potamogeton crispus	Curly pondweed			
Pueraria montana var. lobata	Kudzu			
Rhamnus cathartica	Common buckthorn			
Securigera varia	Crownvetch			
Sesbania herbacea	Bigpod sesbania			
Solanum dulcamara	Climbing nightshade			
Spiraea japonica	Japanese meadowsweet			
Typha angustifolia	Narrowleaf cattail			
Viburnum opulus	European cranberrybush			
Vinca minor	Common periwinkle			
Wisteria sinensis	Chinese wisteria			

Table 2. Overview of invasive exotic plants found on Wilson's Creek National Battlefield. Ecological impact and general management difficulty based on NatureServe I-Rank subranks, Morse et al. 2004. Subranks are given as high (H), medium (M), low (L), insignificant (I), unknown (U), a range of ranks (indicated by /), or not available (--).

Scientific Name	Common Name	Watch List	Park-wide Cover (cres)	Frequency (percent)	Ecological Impact	Management Difficulty
Lespedeza cuneata	Sericea lespedeza	Park-established	479 – 851	44.7	M/L	M/L
Bromus racemosus	Bald brome	Add to park-based	257 – 434	34.0	M/I	U
Maclura pomifera	Osage orange	Park-established	120 – 250	32.5	M/L	L
Bromus inermis	Smooth brome	Park-established	63 – 105	4.0	M	M/L
Lonicera japonica	Japanese honeysuckle	Park-established	48 – 79	37.6	M	H/M
Schedonorus spp.	Fescue species	Park-established	9 – 25	20.8	--	--
Lonicera maackii	Amur honeysuckle	Early detection	5 – 21	1.0	H/M	M
Rosa multiflora	Multiflora rose	Park-established	6 – 17	48.2	L	L
Rhus glabra	Smooth sumac	Park-established	2 – 6	22.8	--	--
Torilis spp.	Hedgeparsley species	Park-established	0.6 – 2.3	25.4	--	--
Bromus sterilis	Poverty brome	Park-established	< 1.0	11.2	M/L	U
Poa spp.	Bluegrass species (incl. Kentucky bluegrass)	Park-established	< 1.0	4.1	--	--
Sorghum halepense	Johnsongrass	Park-established	< 1.0	5.1	M/L	H/M
Dactylis glomerata	Orchardgrass	Park-established	< 0.75	13.2	L/I	M/L
Elaeagnus umbellata	Autumn olive	Early detection	< 0.75	3.6	H	L
Verbascum thapsus	Common mullein	Park-established	< 0.75	15.7	M/L	L
Ailanthus altissima	Tree-of- heaven	Early detection	< 0.5	2.0	M/L	M/L
Carduus nutans	Nodding plumeless thistle	Park-established	< 0.5	2.0	M/I	H/M
Melilotus officinalis	Sweetclover	Park-established	< 0.5	9.6	M	M
Morus alba	White mulberry	Park-established	< 0.5	4.6	M/L	M/L
Securigera varia	Crown vetch	Early detection	< 0.5	2.0	H	L
Celastrus orbiculatus	Oriental bittersweet	Early detection	< 0.25	2.0	M/L	M
Cirsium vulgare	Bull thistle	Early detection	< 0.25	1.5	M/L	M/L
Euonymus alata	Burningbush	Early detection	< 0.25	3.6	L/I	L
Euonymus fortunei	Winter creeper	Early detection	< 0.25	6.6	M	L/I
Bromus tectorum	Cheatgrass	Park-established	< 0.1	1.0	H	H/M
Dipsacus fullonum	Fuller's teasel	Park-established	< 0.1	1.0	L	M/L

Table 2. (continued)

Scientific Name	Common Name	Watch List	Park-wide Cover (cres)	Frequency (percent)	Ecological Impact	Management Difficulty
Humulus japonicus	Japanese hop	Park-established	< 0.1	1.5	--	--
Ligustrum vulgare	Common privet	Park-based	< 0.1	1.5	H/L	H/M
Vinca minor	Common periwinkle	Early detection	< 0.1	1.0	I	U
Arctium minus	Lesser burdock	Park-established	< 0.01	0.5	L/I	M/I
Dioscorea oppositifolia	Chinese yam	Early detection	< 0.01	0.5	M/L	M/I
Miscanthus sinensis	Chinese silvergrass	Early detection	< 0.01	0.5	M/L	H/L
Poa compressa	Canada bluegrass	Park-established	< 0.01	1.0	M/L	H/L
Potentilla recta	Sulphur cinquefoil	Park-established	< 0.01	0.5	H/L	M/L

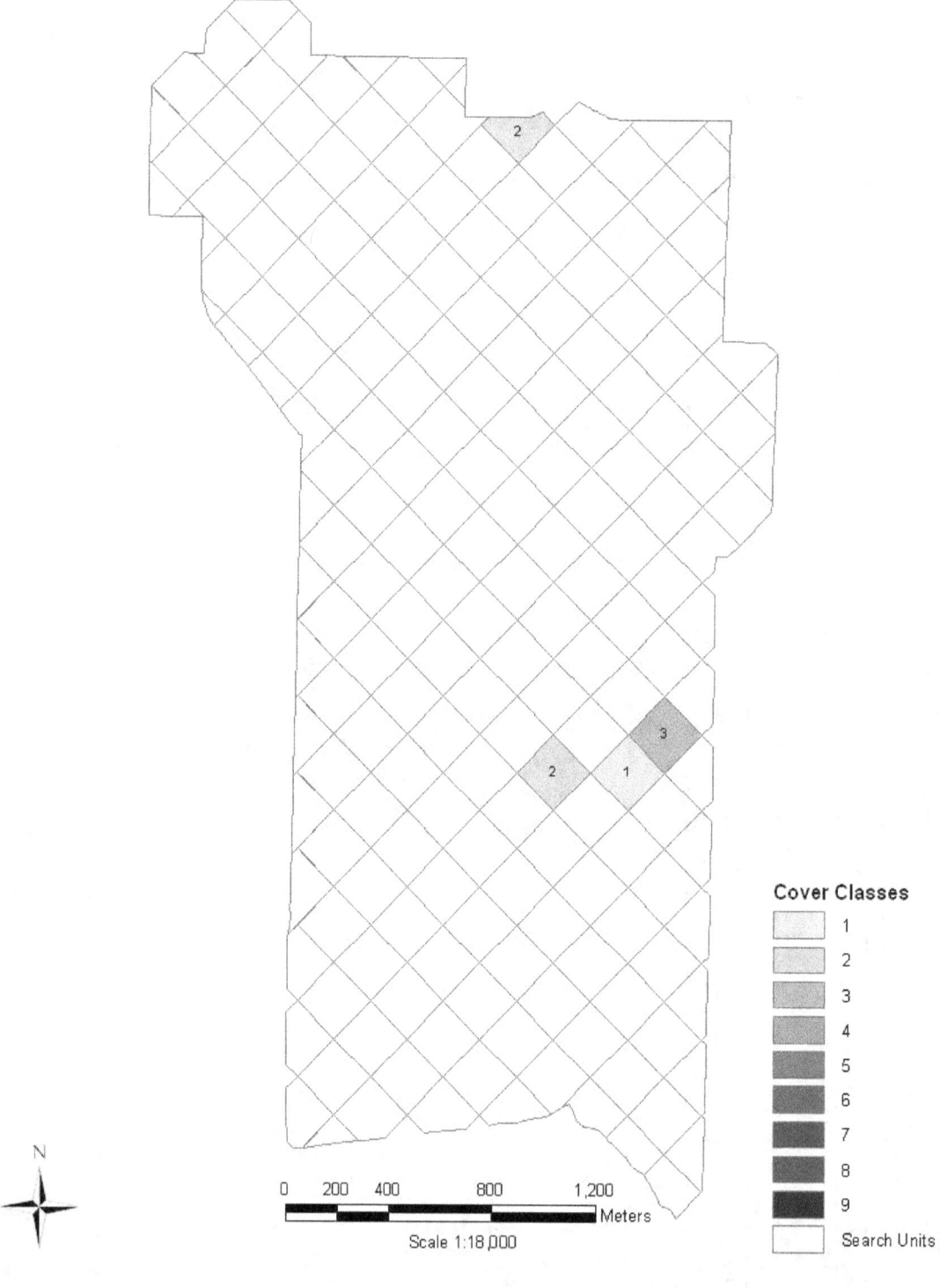

Figure 2. Abundance and distribution of *Ailanthus altissima* (tree-of- heaven) at Wilson's Creek National Battlefield, 2006. Cover classes are as follows: 1=0.1-0.9 m^2, 2=1-9.9 m^2, 3=10-49.9 m^2, 4= 50-99.9 m^2, 5=100-499.9 m^2, 6= 499.9-999.9 m^2, 7=1,000-4,999.9 m^2, 8=5,000-9,999.9 m^2, and 9=10,000-14,999.9. See figure 1 for areas not searched.

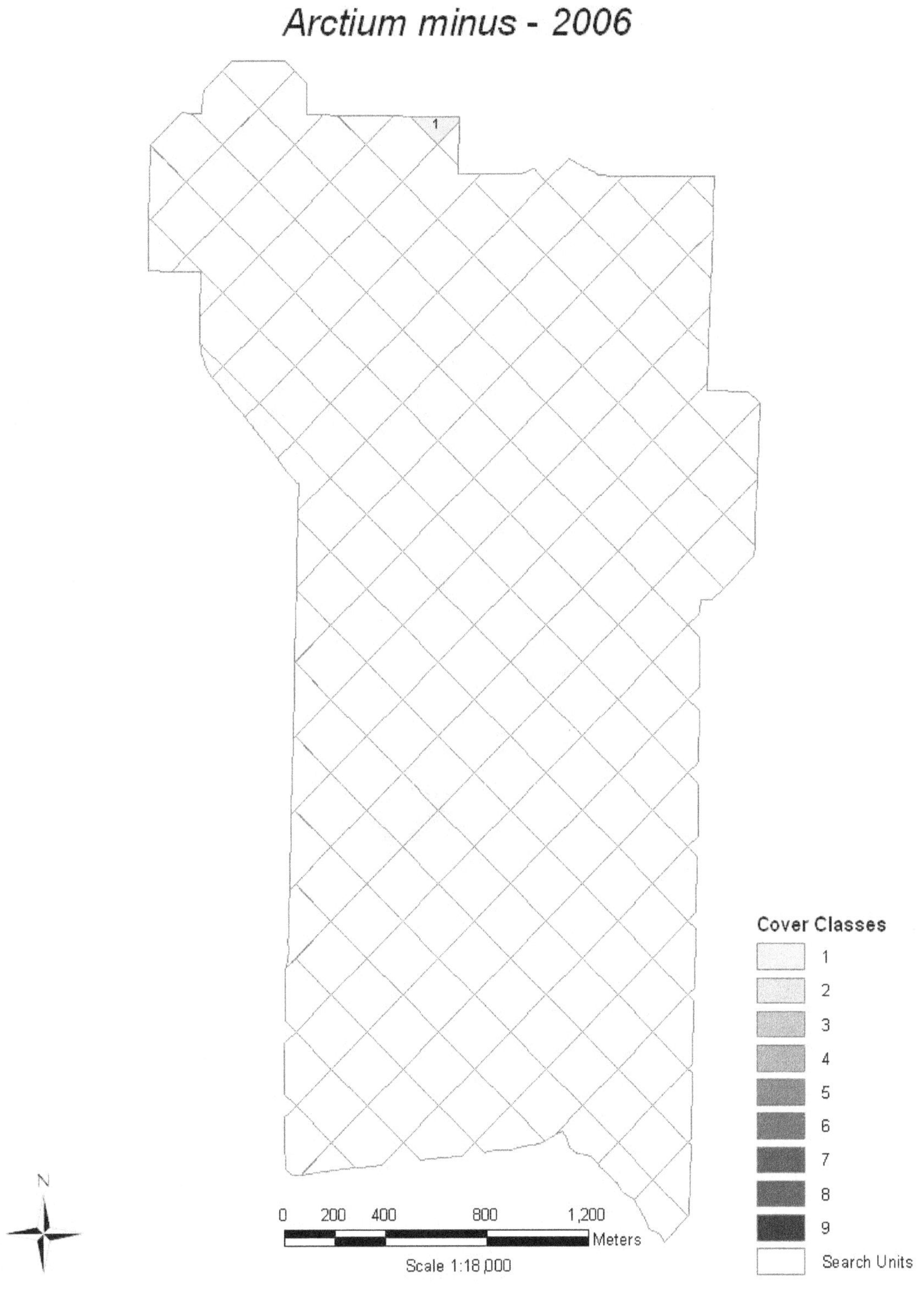

Figure 3. Abundance and distribution of *Arctium minus* (lesser burdock) at Wilson's Creek National Battlefield, 2006. Cover classes are as follows: 1=0.1-0.9 m^2, 2=1-9.9 m^2, 3=10-49.9 m^2, 4= 50-99.9 m^2, 5=100-499.9 m^2, 6= 499.9-999.9 m^2, 7=1,000-4,999.9 m^2, 8=5,000-9,999.9 m^2, and 9=10,000-14,999.9. See figure 1 for areas not searched.

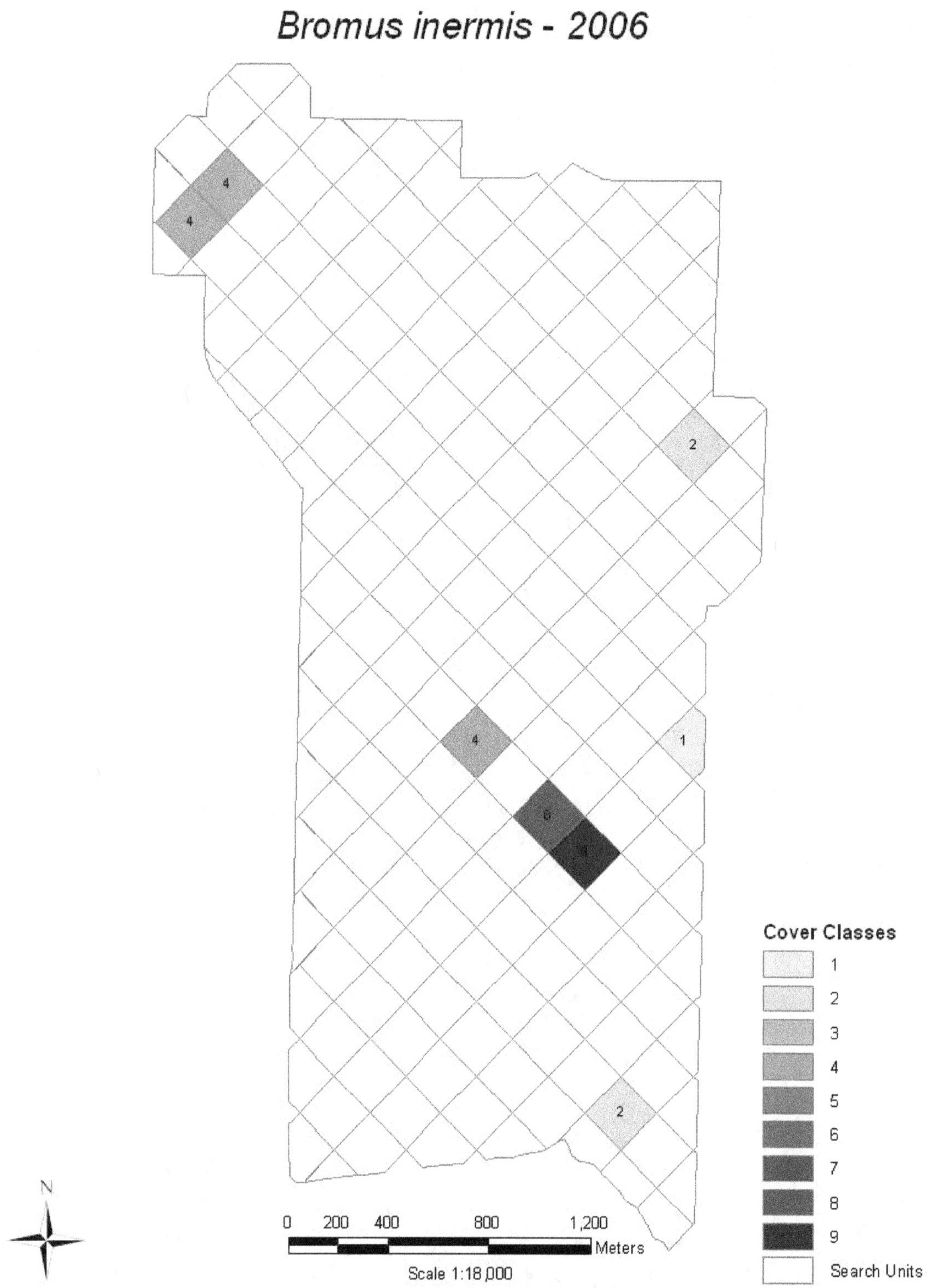

Bromus inermis - 2006

Figure 4. Abundance and distribution of *Bromus inermis* (smooth brome) at Wilson's Creek National Battlefield, 2006. Cover classes are as follows: 1=0.1-0.9 m^2, 2=1-9.9 m^2, 3=10-49.9 m^2, 4= 50-99.9 m^2, 5=100-499.9 m^2, 6= 499.9-999.9 m^2, 7=1,000-4,999.9 m^2, 8=5,000-9,999.9 m^2, and 9=10,000-14,999.9. See figure 1 for areas not searched.

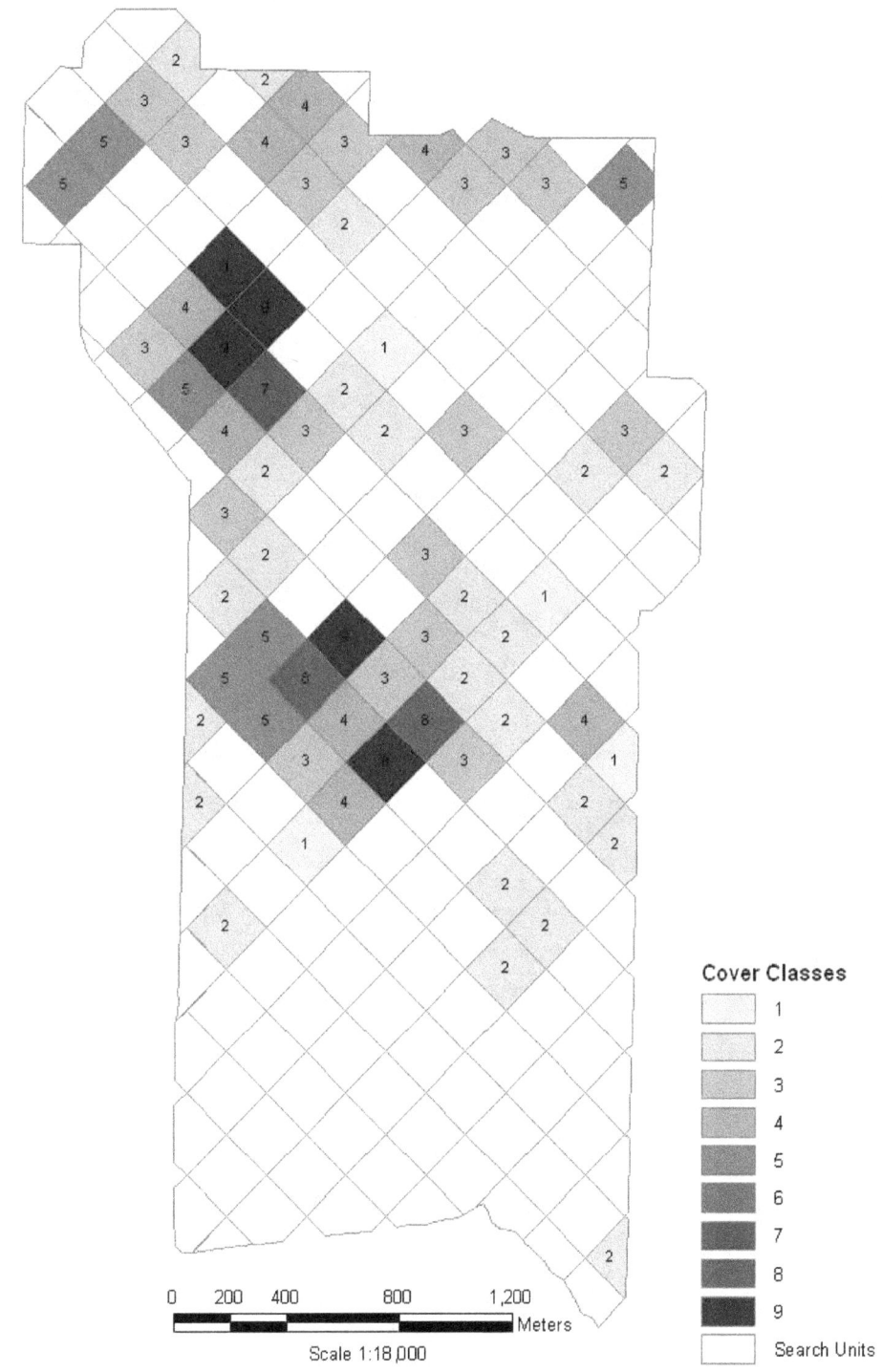

Figure 5. Abundance and distribution of *Bromus racemosus* (bald brome) at Wilson's Creek National Battlefield, 2006. Cover classes are as follows: 1=0.1-0.9 m², 2=1-9.9 m², 3=10-49.9 m², 4= 50-99.9 m², 5=100-499.9 m², 6= 499.9-999.9 m², 7=1,000-4,999.9 m², 8=5,000-9,999.9 m², and 9=10,000-14,999.9. See figure 1 for areas not searched.

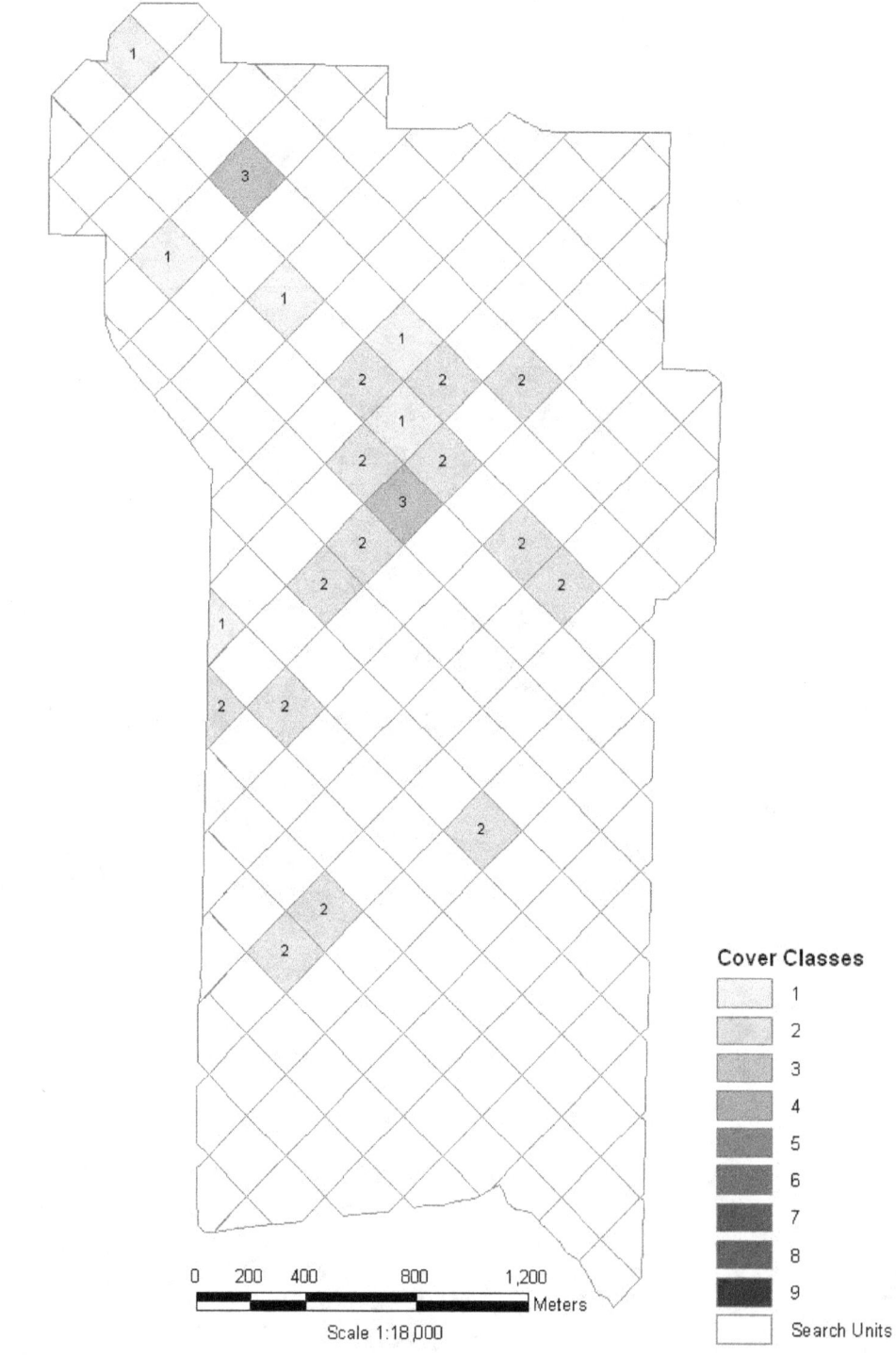

Bromus sterilis - 2006

Cover Classes
1
2
3
4
5
6
7
8
9
Search Units

0 200 400 800 1,200 Meters
Scale 1:18,000

N

Figure 6. Abundance and distribution of *Bromus sterilis* (poverty brome) at Wilson's Creek National Battlefield, 2006. Cover classes are as follows: 1=0.1-0.9 m², 2=1-9.9 m², 3=10-49.9 m², 4= 50-99.9 m², 5=100-499.9 m², 6= 499.9-999.9 m², 7=1,000-4,999.9 m², 5,000-9,999.9 m², and 9=10,000-14,999.9. See figure 1 for areas not searched.

16

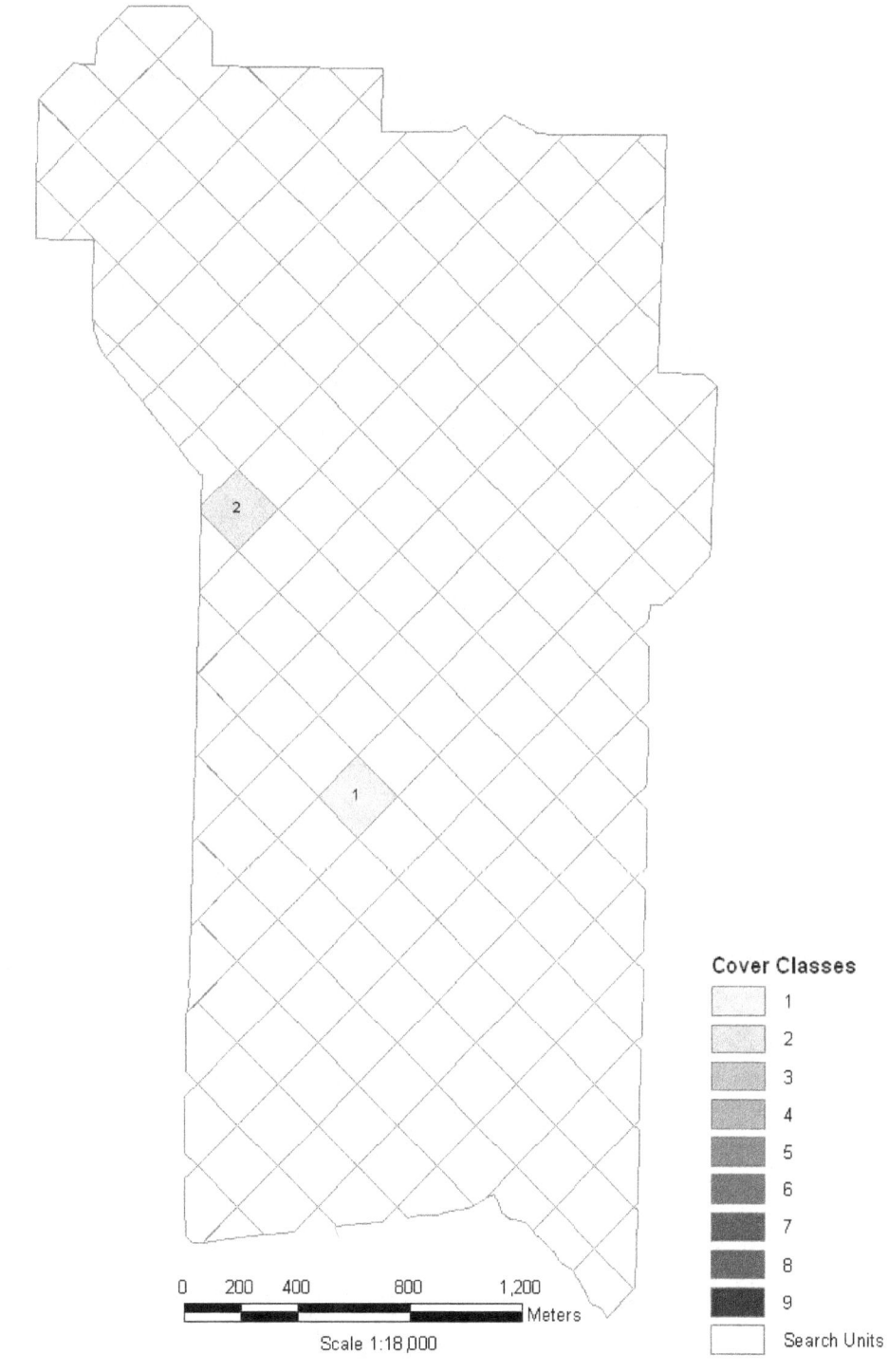

Figure 7. Abundance and distribution of *Bromus tectorum* (cheatgrass) at Wilson's Creek National Battlefield, 2006. Cover classes are as follows: 1=0.1-0.9 m^2, 2=1-9.9 m^2, 3=10-49.9 m^2, 4= 50-99.9 m^2, 5=100-499.9 m^2, 6= 499.9-999.9 m^2, 7=1,000-4,999.9 m^2, 5,000-9,999.9 m^2, and 9=10,000-14,999.9. See figure 1 for areas not searched.

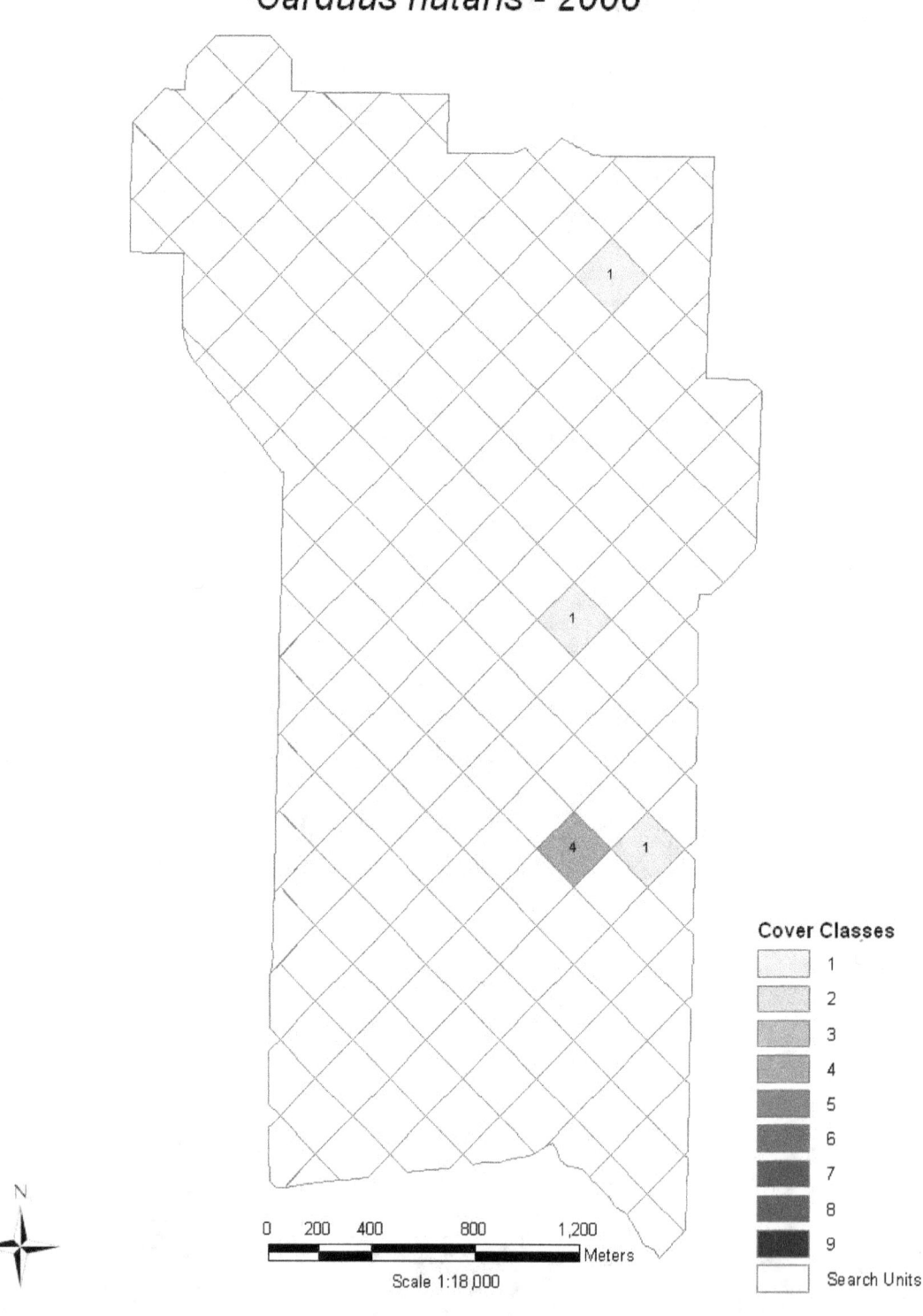

Figure 8. Abundance and distribution of *Carduus nutans* (nodding plumeless thistle) at Wilson's Creek National Battlefield, 2006. Cover classes are as follows: 1=0.1-0.9 m², 2=1-9.9 m², 3=10-49.9 m², 4= 50-99.9 m², 5=100-499.9 m², 6= 499.9-999.9 m², 7=1,000-4,999.9 m², 5,000-9,999.9 m², and 9=10,000-14,999.9. See figure 1 for areas not searched.

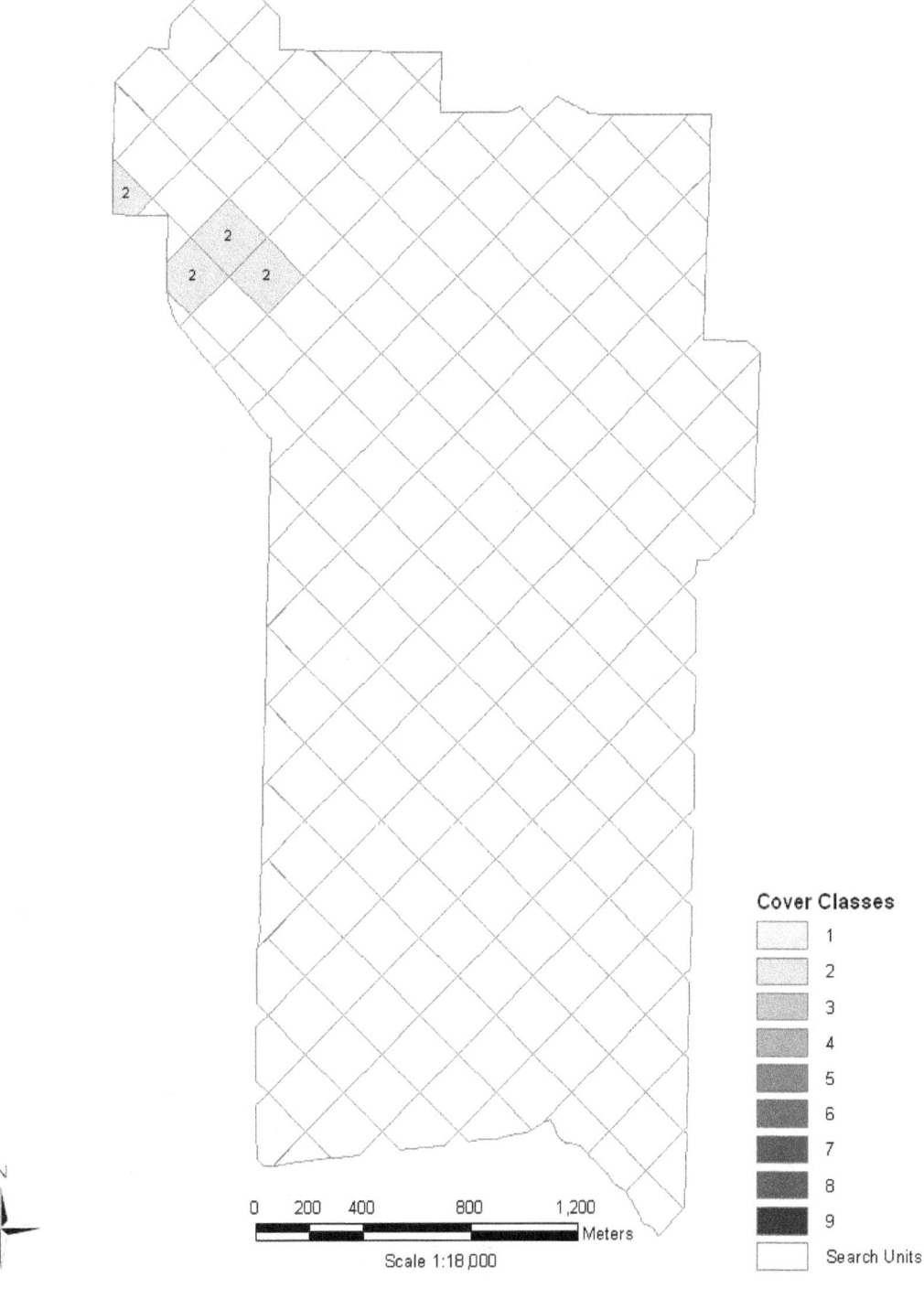

Figure 9. Abundance and distribution of *Celastrus orbiculatus* (Oriental bittersweet) at Wilson's Creek National Battlefield, 2006. Cover classes are as follows: 1=0.1-0.9 m^2, 2=1-9.9 m^2, 3=10-49.9 m^2, 4= 50-99.9 m^2, 5=100-499.9 m^2, 6= 499.9-999.9 m^2, 7=1,000-4,999.9 m^2, 5,000-9,999.9 m^2, and 9=10,000-14,999.9. See figure 1 for areas not searched.

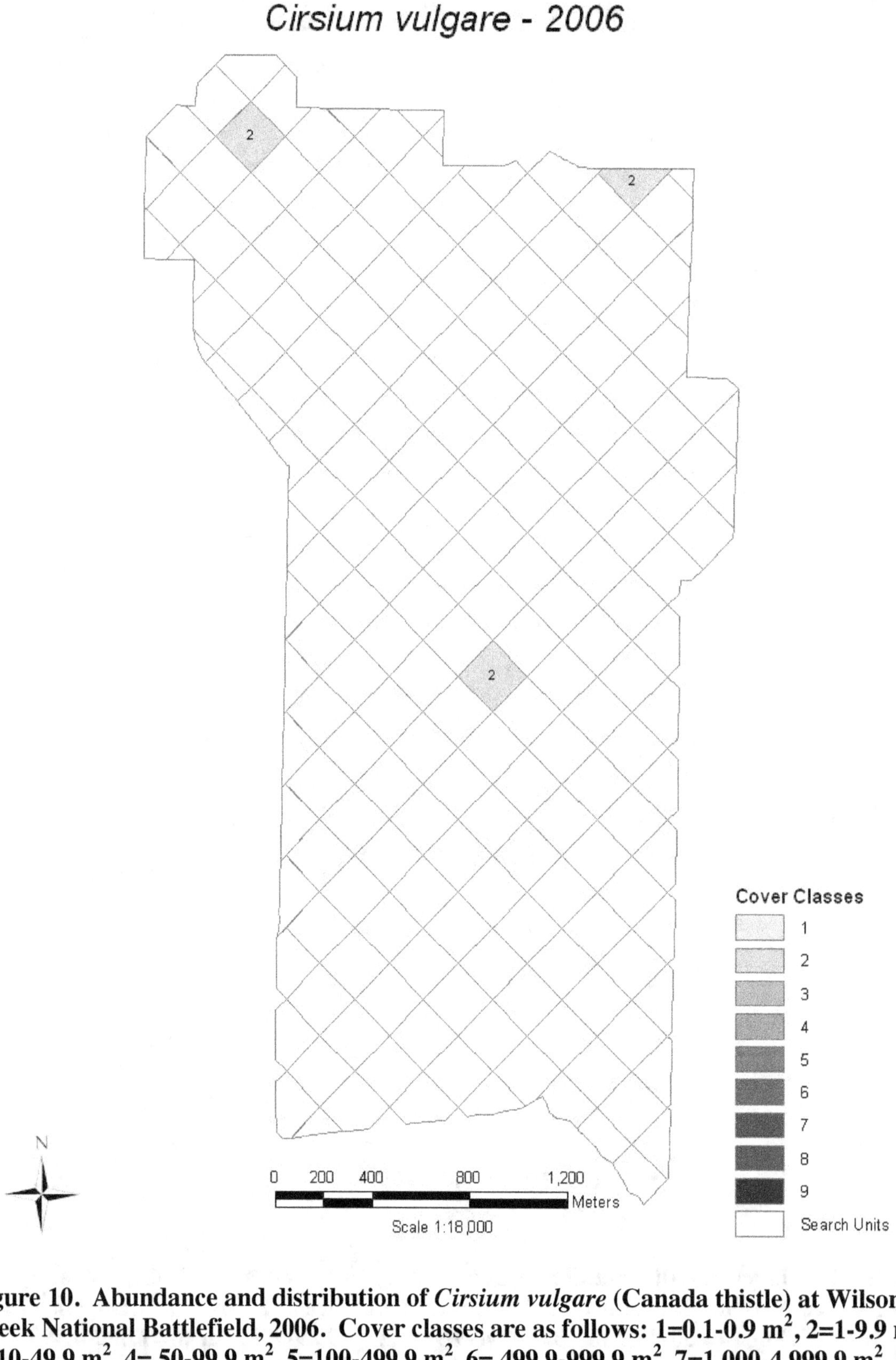

Figure 10. Abundance and distribution of *Cirsium vulgare* (Canada thistle) at Wilson's Creek National Battlefield, 2006. Cover classes are as follows: 1=0.1-0.9 m², 2=1-9.9 m², 3=10-49.9 m², 4= 50-99.9 m², 5=100-499.9 m², 6= 499.9-999.9 m², 7=1,000-4,999.9 m², 5,000-9,999.9 m², and 9=10,000-14,999.9. See figure 1 for areas not searched.

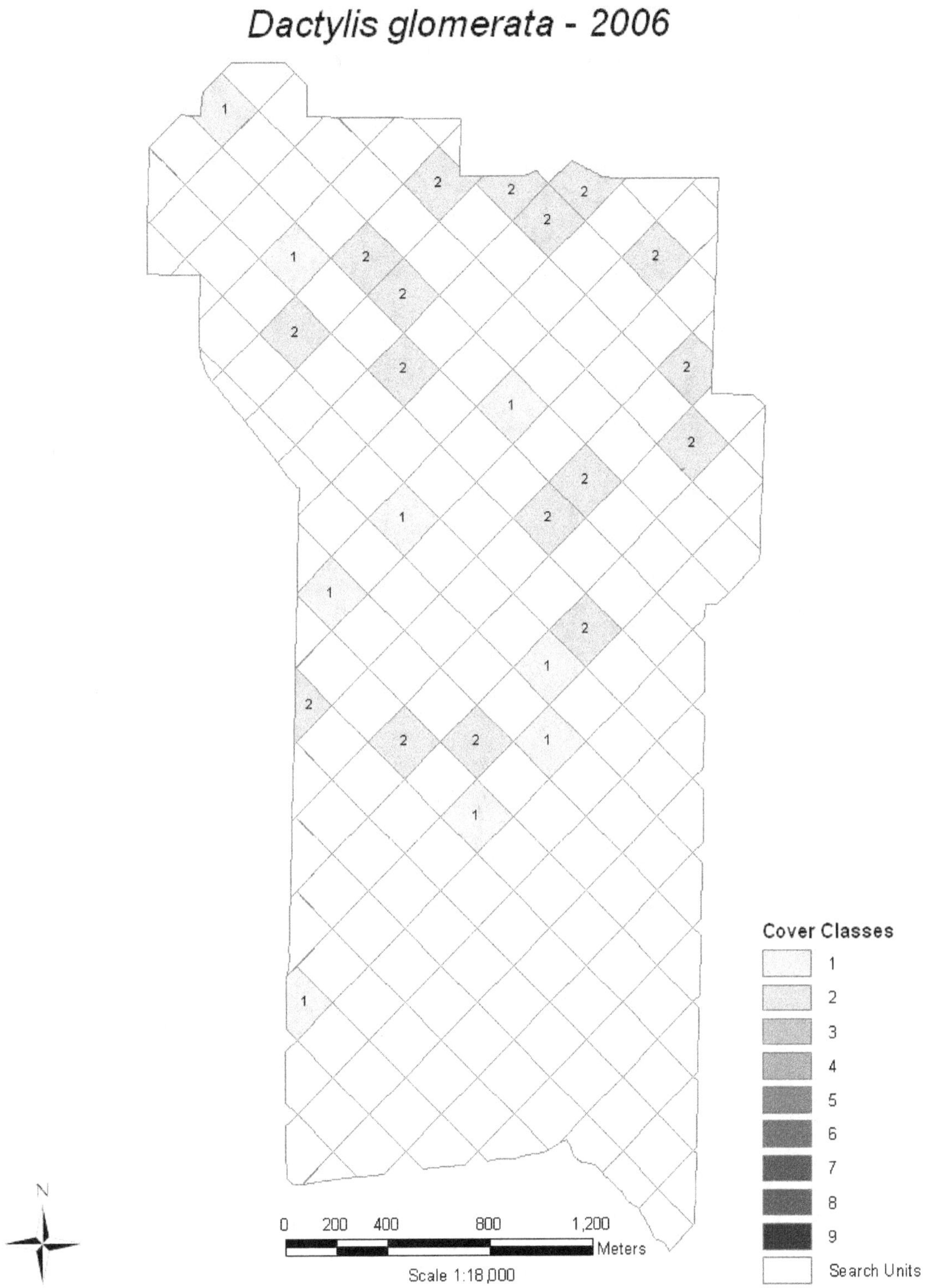

Figure 11. Abundance and distribution of *Dactylis glomerata* (orchardgrass) at Wilson's Creek National Battlefield, 2006. Cover classes are as follows: 1=0.1-0.9 m^2, 2=1-9.9 m^2, 3=10-49.9 m^2, 4= 50-99.9 m^2, 5=100-499.9 m^2, 6= 499.9-999.9 m^2, 7=1,000-4,999.9 m^2, 5,000-9,999.9 m^2, and 9=10,000-14,999.9. See figure 1 for areas not searched.

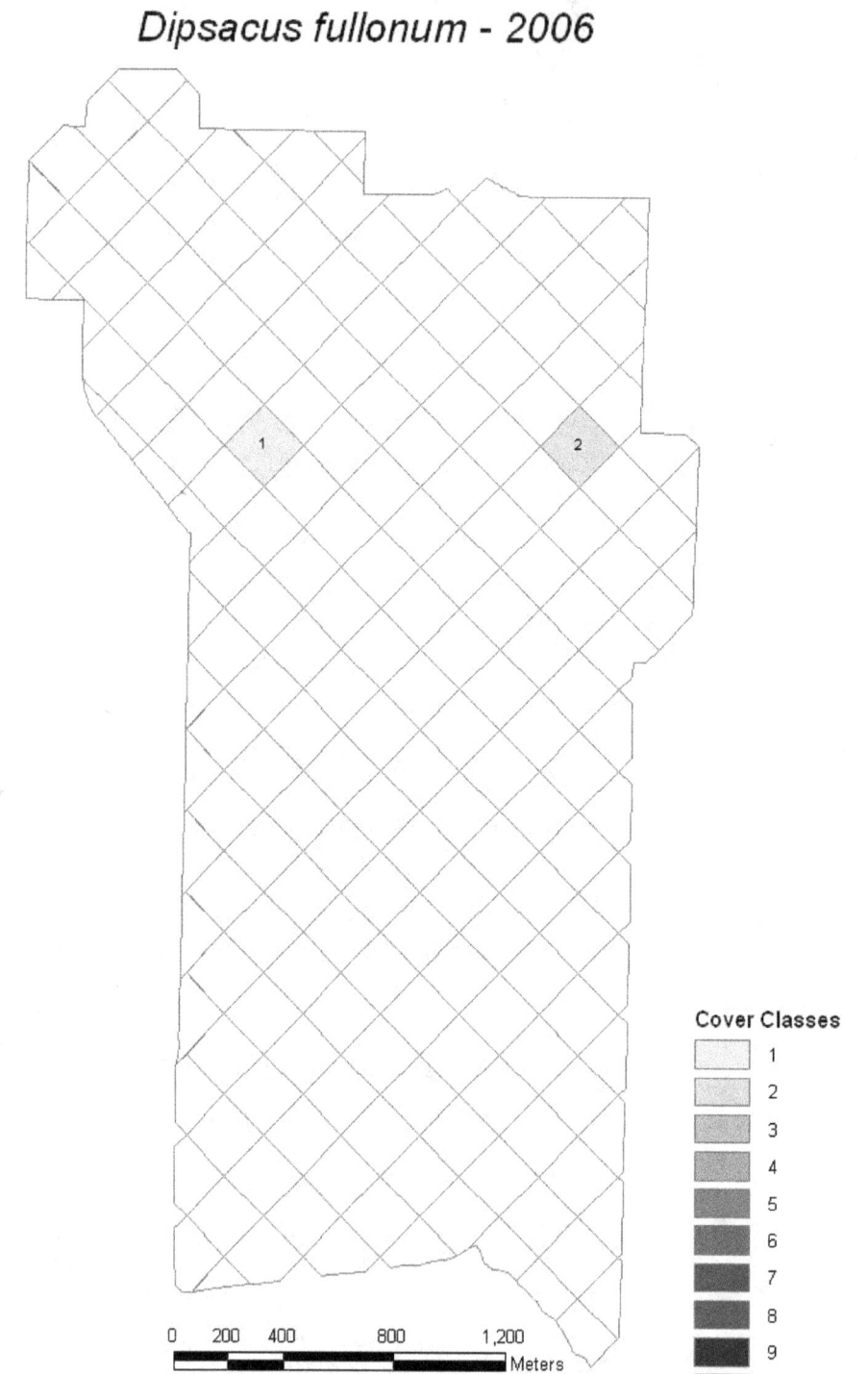

Figure 12. Abundance and distribution of *Dipsacus fullonum* (Fuller's teasel) at Wilson's Creek National Battlefield, 2006. Cover classes are as follows: 1=0.1-0.9 m^2, 2=1-9.9 m^2, 3=10-49.9 m^2, 4= 50-99.9 m^2, 5=100-499.9 m^2, 6= 499.9-999.9 m^2, 7=1,000-4,999.9 m^2, 5,000-9,999.9 m^2, and 9=10,000-14,999.9. See figure 1 for areas not searched.

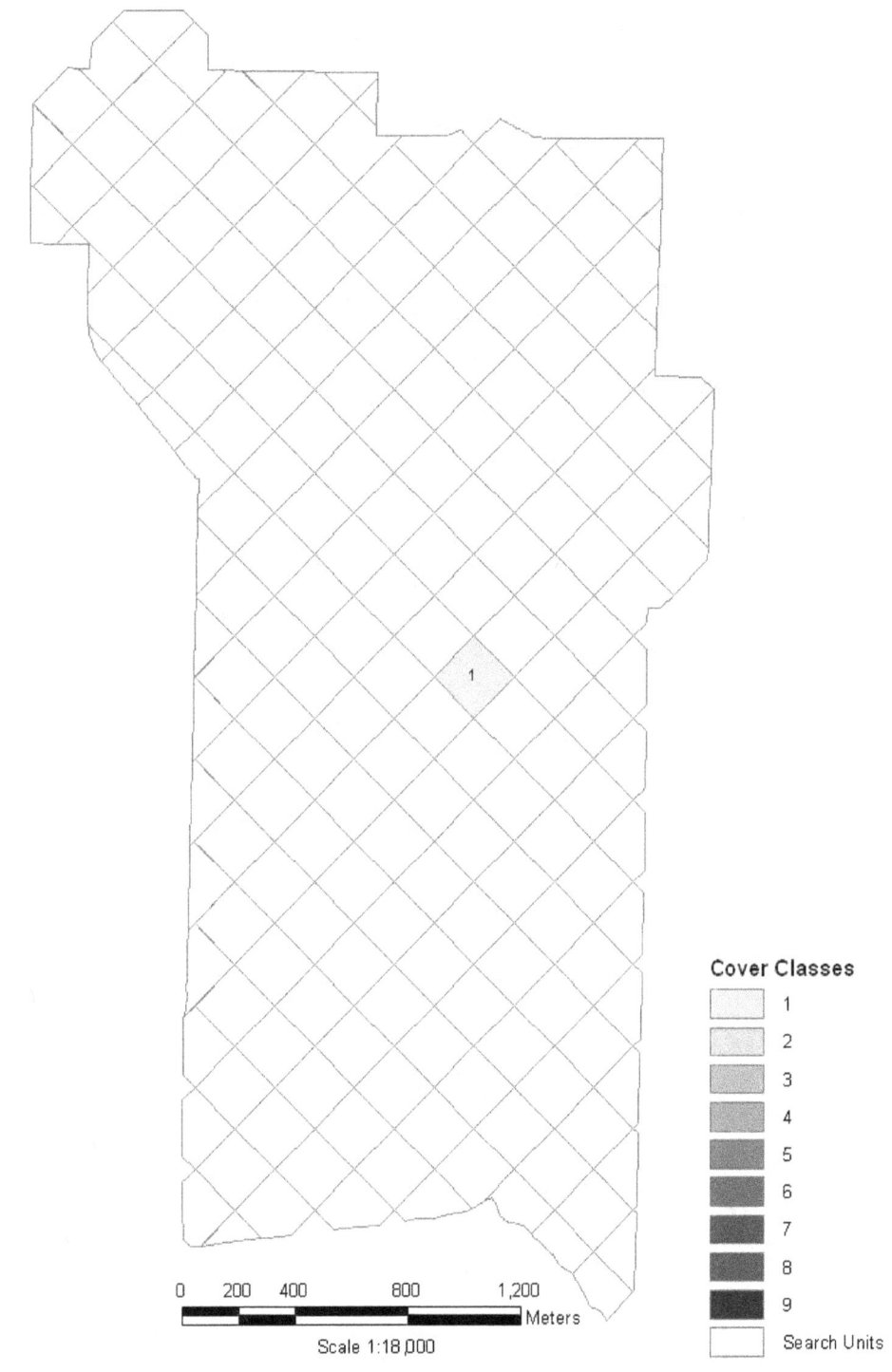

Dioscorea oppositifolia - 2006

Cover Classes

1
2
3
4
5
6
7
8
9
Search Units

0   200   400   800   1,200
Meters
Scale 1:18,000

N

Figure 13. Abundance and distribution of *Dioscorea oppositifolia* (Chinese yam) at Wilson's Creek National Battlefield, 2006. Cover classes are as follows: 1=0.1-0.9 m², 2=1-9.9 m², 3=10-49.9 m², 4= 50-99.9 m², 5=100-499.9 m², 6= 499.9-999.9 m², 7=1,000-4,999.9 m², 5,000-9,999.9 m², and 9=10,000-14,999.9. See figure 1 for areas not searched.

Elaeagnus umbellata - 2006

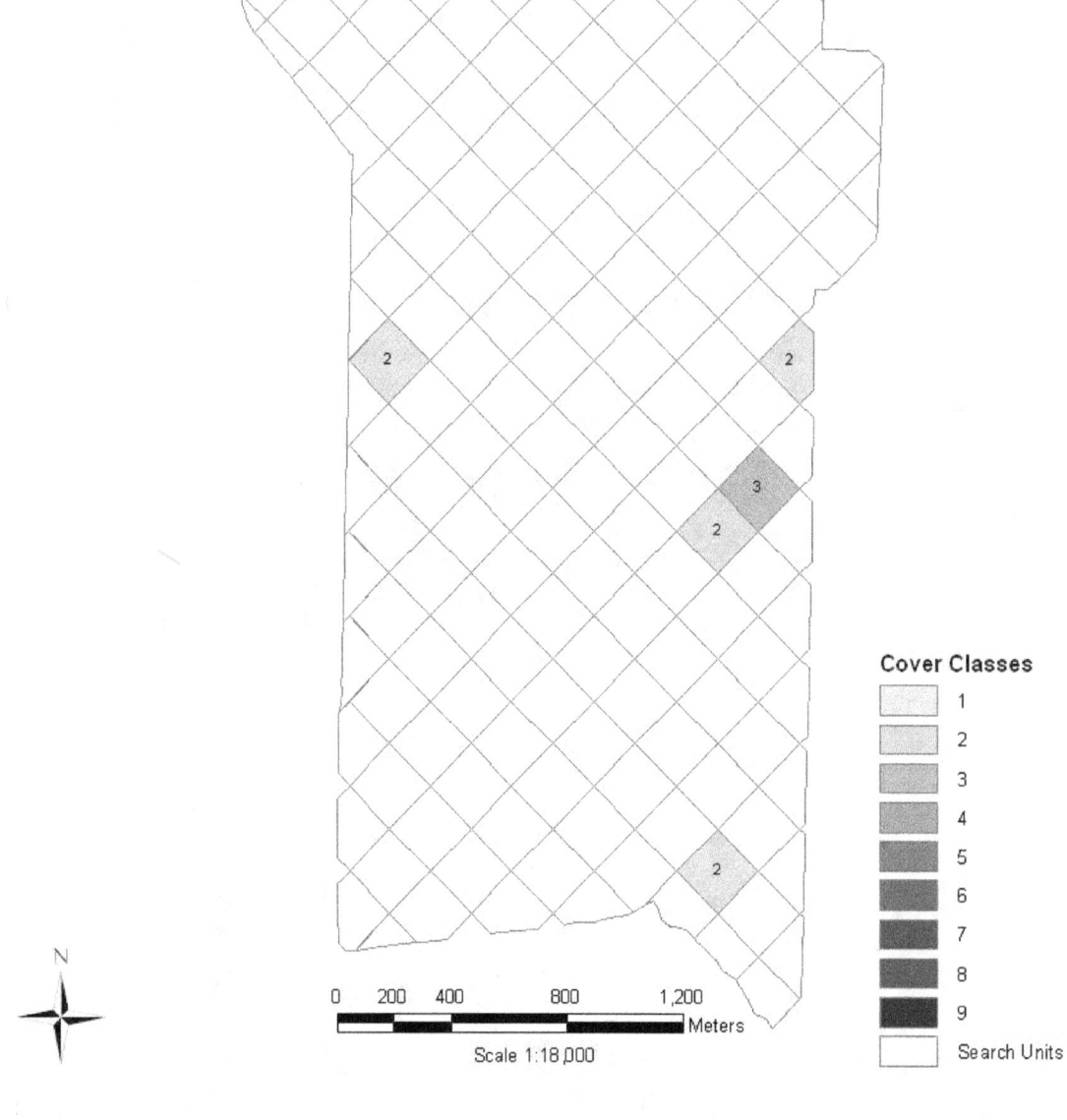

Figure 14. Abundance and distribution of *Elaeagnus umbellata* (Autumn olive) at Wilson's Creek National Battlefield, 2006. Cover classes are as follows: 1=0.1-0.9 m², 2=1-9.9 m², 3=10-49.9 m², 4= 50-99.9 m², 5=100-499.9 m², 6= 499.9-999.9 m², 7=1,000-4,999.9 m², 5,000-9,999.9 m², and 9=10,000-14,999.9. See figure 1 for areas not searched.

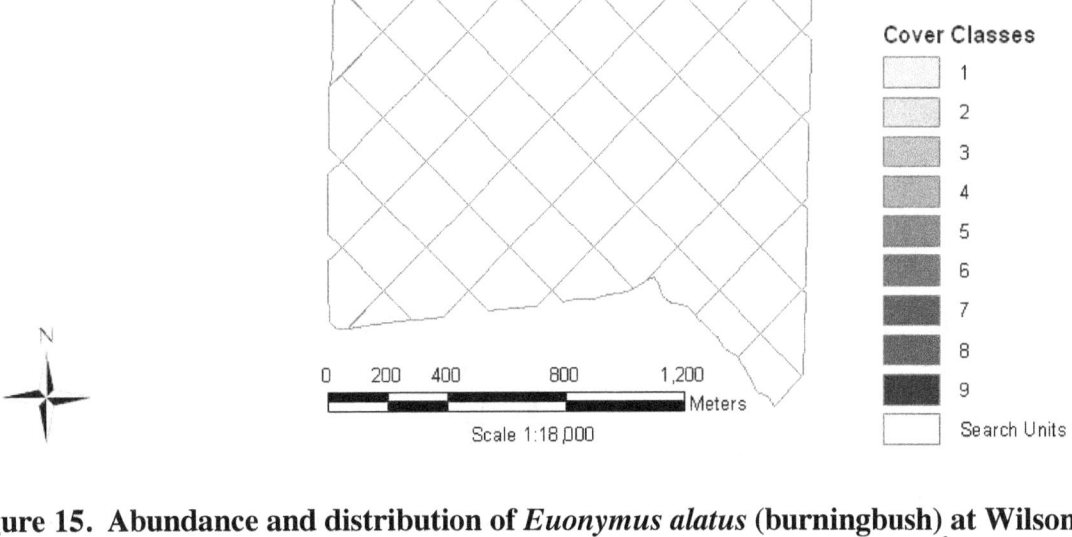

Figure 15. Abundance and distribution of *Euonymus alatus* (burningbush) at Wilson's Creek National Battlefield, 2006. Cover classes are as follows: 1=0.1-0.9 m², 2=1-9.9 m², 3=10-49.9 m², 4= 50-99.9 m², 5=100-499.9 m², 6= 499.9-999.9 m², 7=1,000-4,999.9 m², 5,000-9,999.9 m², and 9=10,000-14,999.9. See figure 1 for areas not searched.

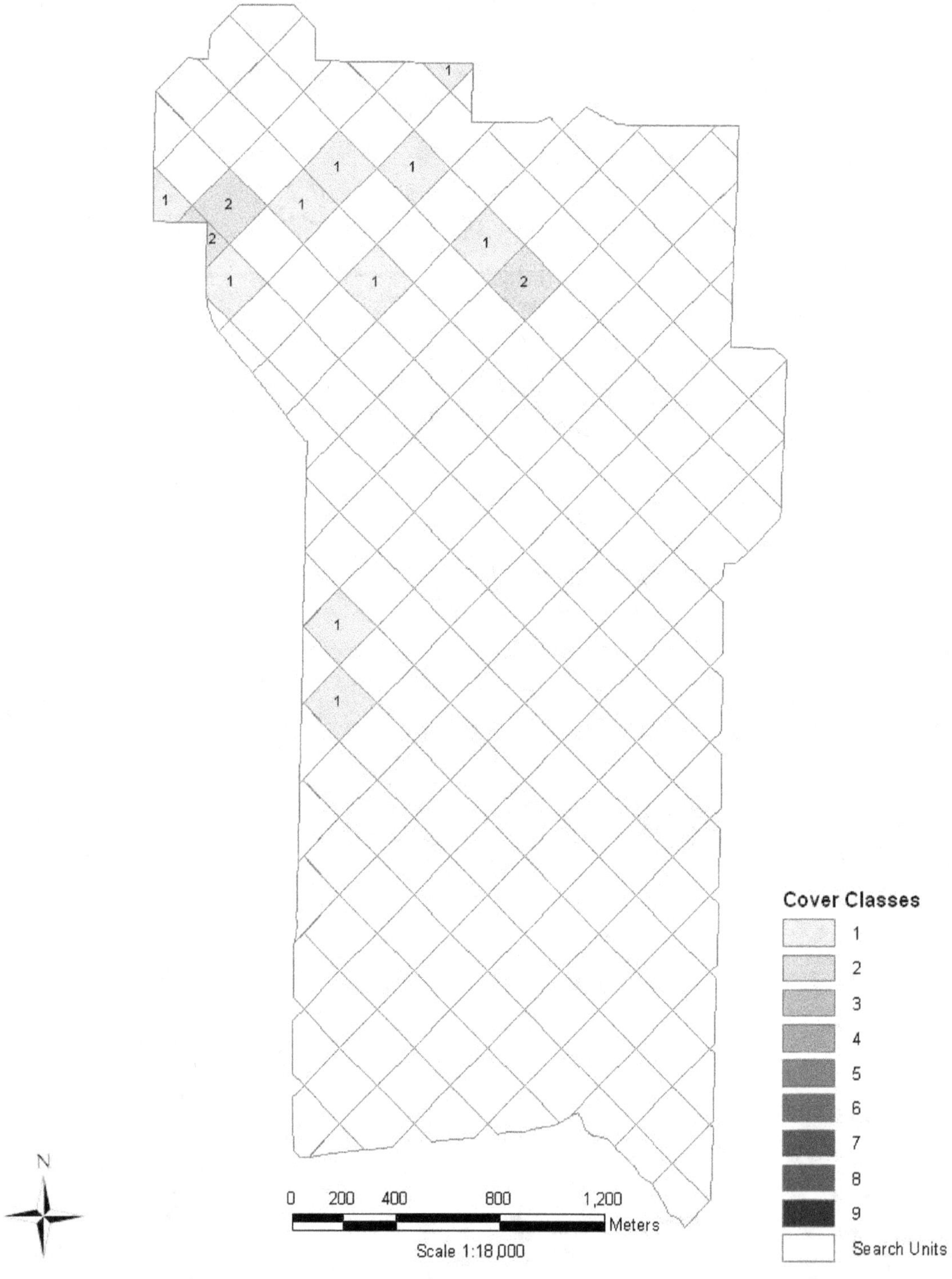

Figure 16. Abundance and distribution of *Euonymus fortunei* (winter creeper) at Wilson's Creek National Battlefield, 2006. Cover classes are as follows: 1=0.1-0.9 m², 2=1-9.9 m², 3=10-49.9 m², 4= 50-99.9 m², 5=100-499.9 m², 6= 499.9-999.9 m², 7=1,000-4,999.9 m², 5,000-9,999.9 m², and 9=10,000-14,999.9. See figure 1 for areas not searched.

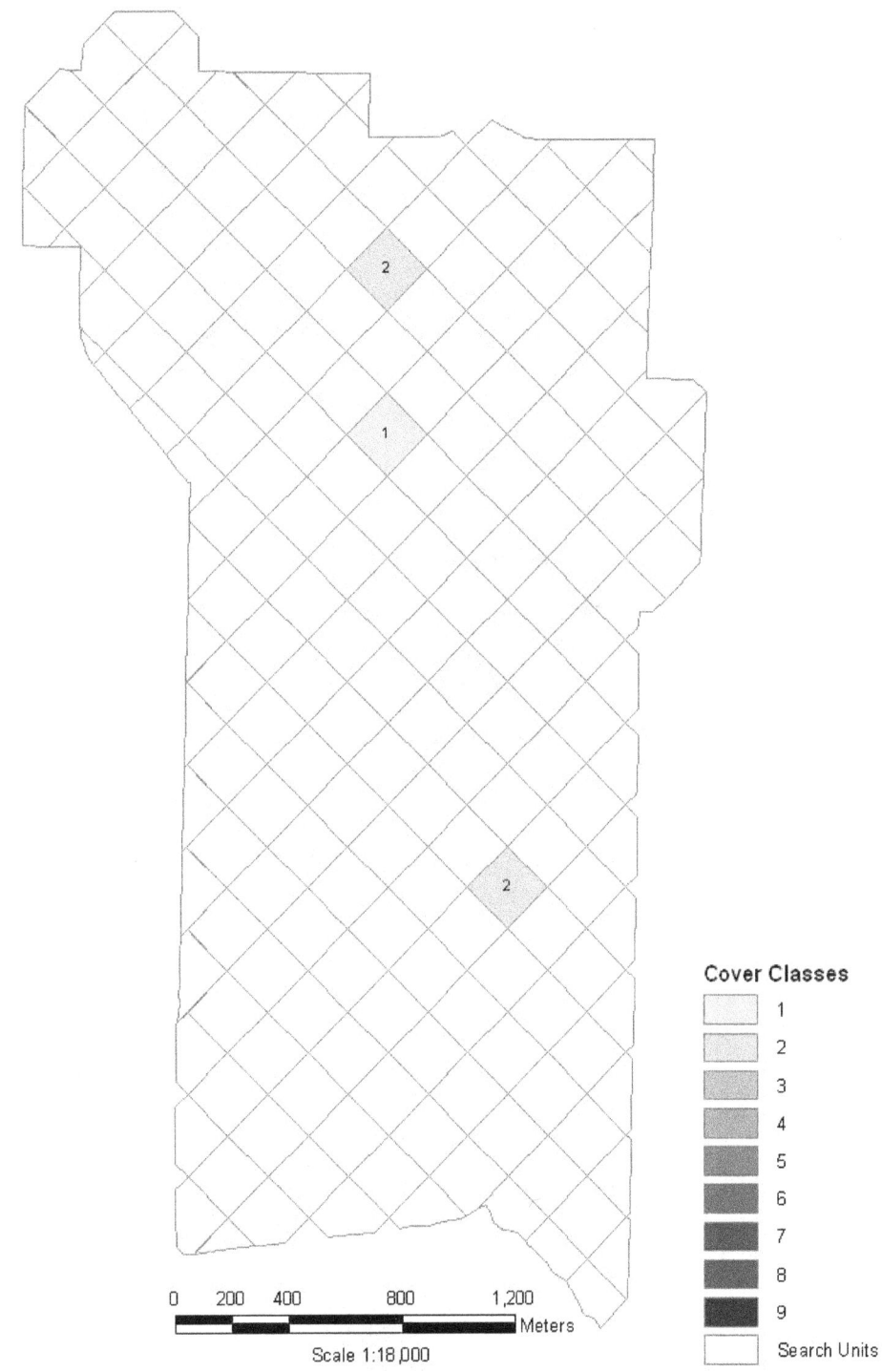

Figure 17. Abundance and distribution of *Humulus japonicus* (Japanese hop) at Wilson's Creek National Battlefield, 2006. Cover classes are as follows: 1=0.1-0.9 m^2, 2=1-9.9 m^2, 3=10-49.9 m^2, 4= 50-99.9 m^2, 5=100-499.9 m^2, 6= 499.9-999.9 m^2, 7=1000-4999.9 m^2, 8=5000-9999.9 m^2, and 9=10,000-14999.9. See figure 1 for areas not searched.

Figure 18. Abundance and distribution of *Lespedeza cuneata* (sericea lespedeza) at Wilson's Creek National Battlefield, 2006. Cover classes are as follows: 1=0.1-0.9 m^2, 2=1-9.9 m^2, 3=10-49.9 m^2, 4= 50-99.9 m^2, 5=100-499.9 m^2, 6= 499.9-999.9 m^2, 7=1,000-4,999.9 m^2, 5,000-9,999.9 m^2, and 9=10,000-14,999.9. See figure 1 for areas not searched.

Ligustrum vulgare - 2006

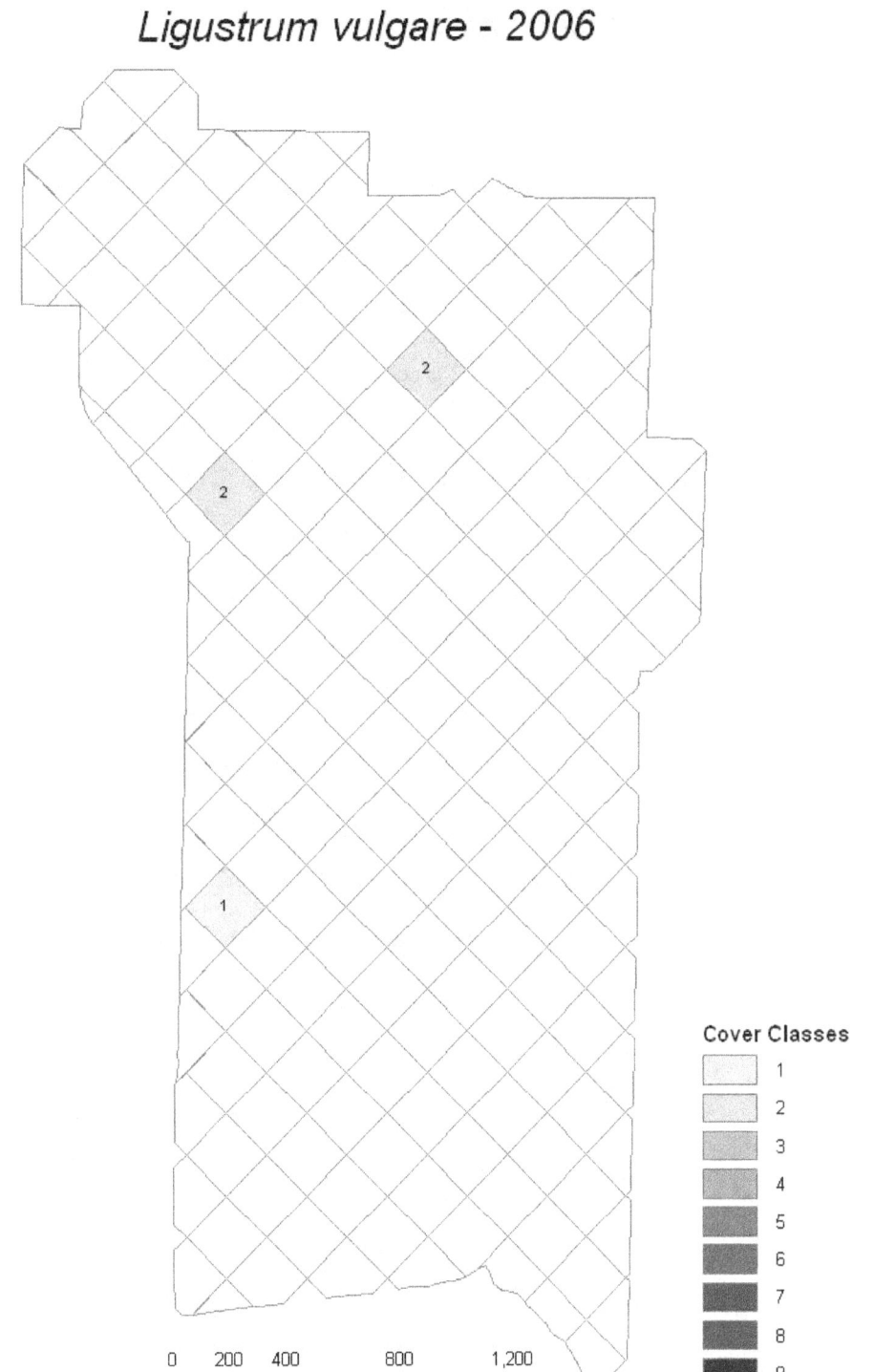

Figure 19. Abundance and distribution of *Ligustrum vulgare* (European privet) at Wilson's Creek National Battlefield, 2006. Cover classes are as follows: 1=0.1-0.9 m², 2=1-9.9 m², 3=10-49.9 m², 4= 50-99.9 m², 5=100-499.9 m², 6= 499.9-999.9 m², 7=1,000-4,999.9 m², 5,000-9,999.9 m², and 9=10,000-14,999.9. See figure 1 for areas not searched.

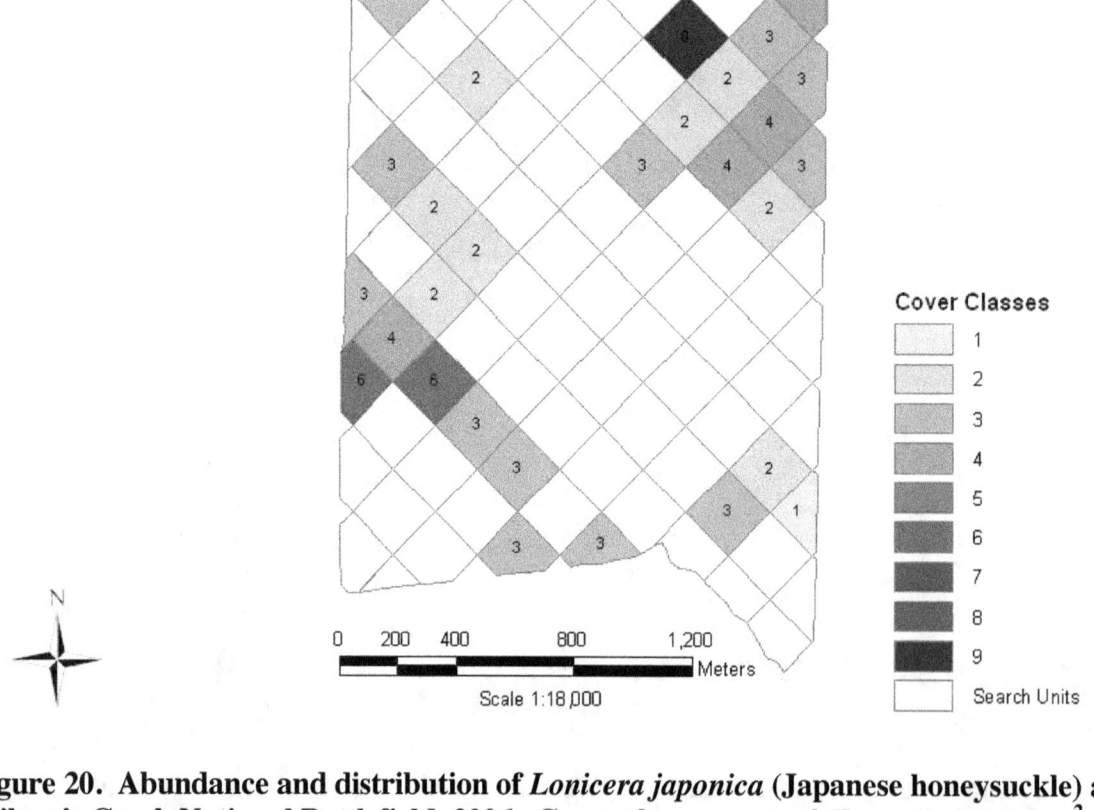

Figure 20. Abundance and distribution of *Lonicera japonica* (Japanese honeysuckle) at Wilson's Creek National Battlefield, 2006. Cover classes are as follows: 1=0.1-0.9 m², 2=1-9.9 m², 3=10-49.9 m², 4= 50-99.9 m², 5=100-499.9 m², 6= 499.9-999.9 m², 7=1,000-4,999.9 m², 5,000-9,999.9 m², and 9=10,000-14,999.9. See figure 1 for areas not searched.

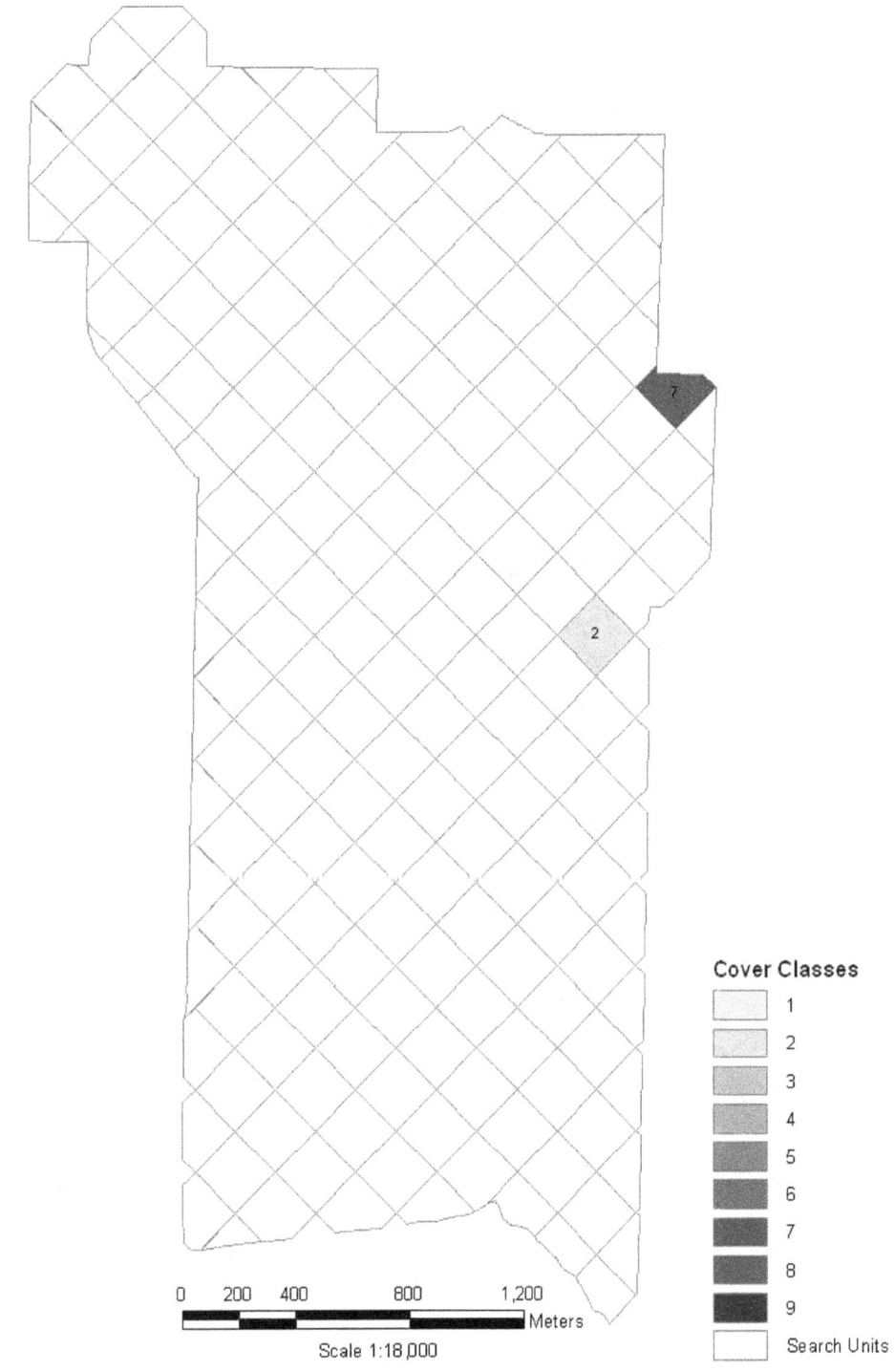

Figure 21. Abundance and distribution of *Lonicera maackii* (amur honeysuckle) at Wilson's Creek National Battlefield, 2006. Cover classes are as follows: 1=0.1-0.9 m², 2=1-9.9 m², 3=10-49.9 m², 4= 50-99.9 m², 5=100-499.9 m², 6= 499.9-999.9 m², 7=1,000-4,999.9 m², 5,000-9,999.9 m², and 9=10,000-14,999.9. See figure 1 for areas not searched.

Figure 22. Abundance and distribution of *Maclura pomifera* (Osage orange) at Wilson's Creek National Battlefield, 2006. Cover classes are as follows: 1=0.1-0.9 m^2, 2=1-9.9 m^2, 3=10-49.9 m^2, 4= 50-99.9 m^2, 5=100-499.9 m^2, 6= 499.9-999.9 m^2, 7=1,000-4,999.9 m^2, 5,000-9,999.9 m^2, and 9=10,000-14,999.9. See figure 1 for areas not searched.

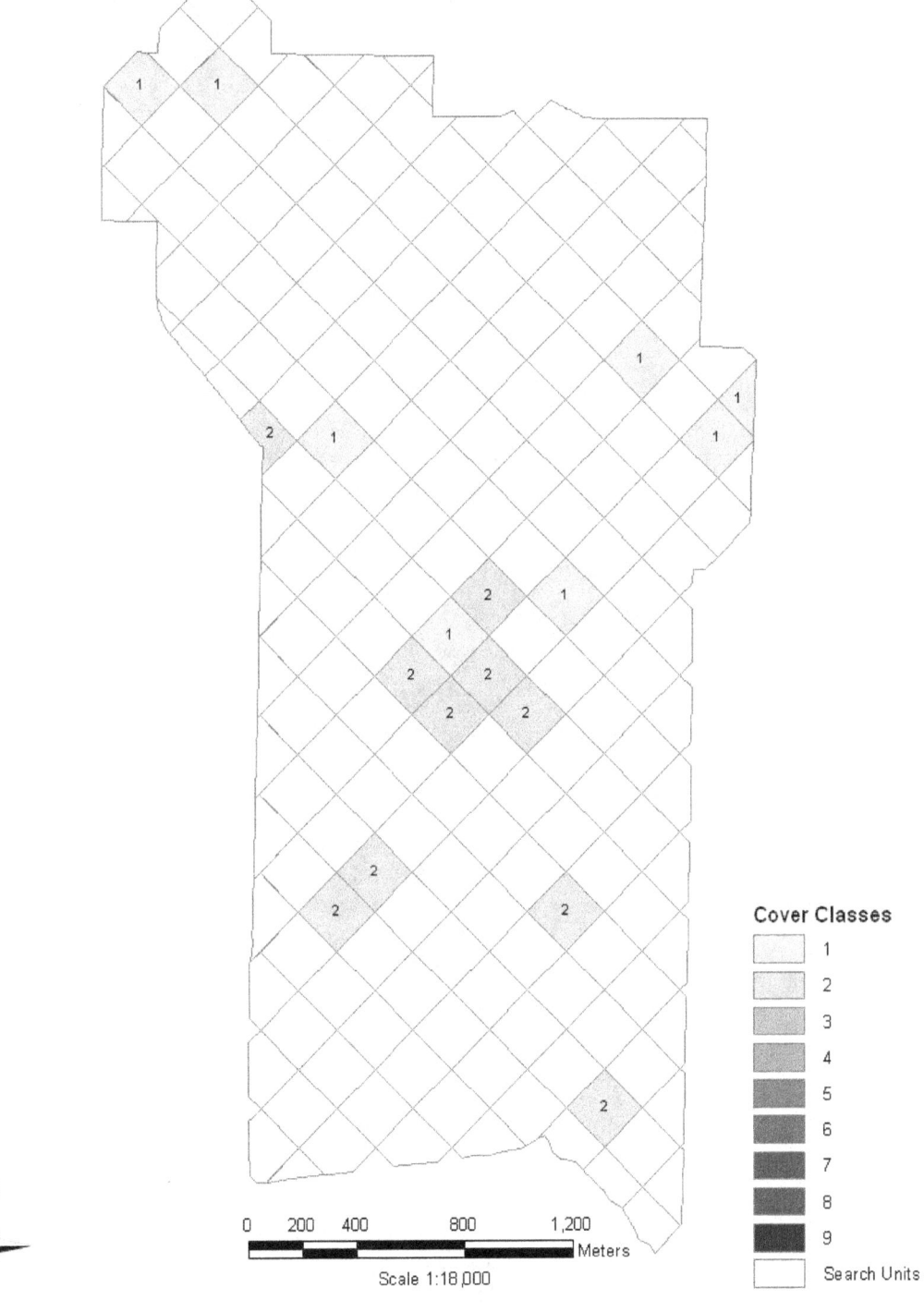

Figure 23. Abundance and distribution of *Melilotus officinalis* (sweetclover) at Wilson's Creek National Battlefield, 2006. Cover classes are as follows: 1=0.1-0.9 m², 2=1-9.9 m², 3=10-49.9 m², 4= 50-99.9 m², 5=100-499.9 m², 6= 499.9-999.9 m², 7=1,000-4,999.9 m², 5,000-9,999.9 m², and 9=10,000-14,999.9. See figure 1 for areas not searched.

Miscanthus sinensis - 2006

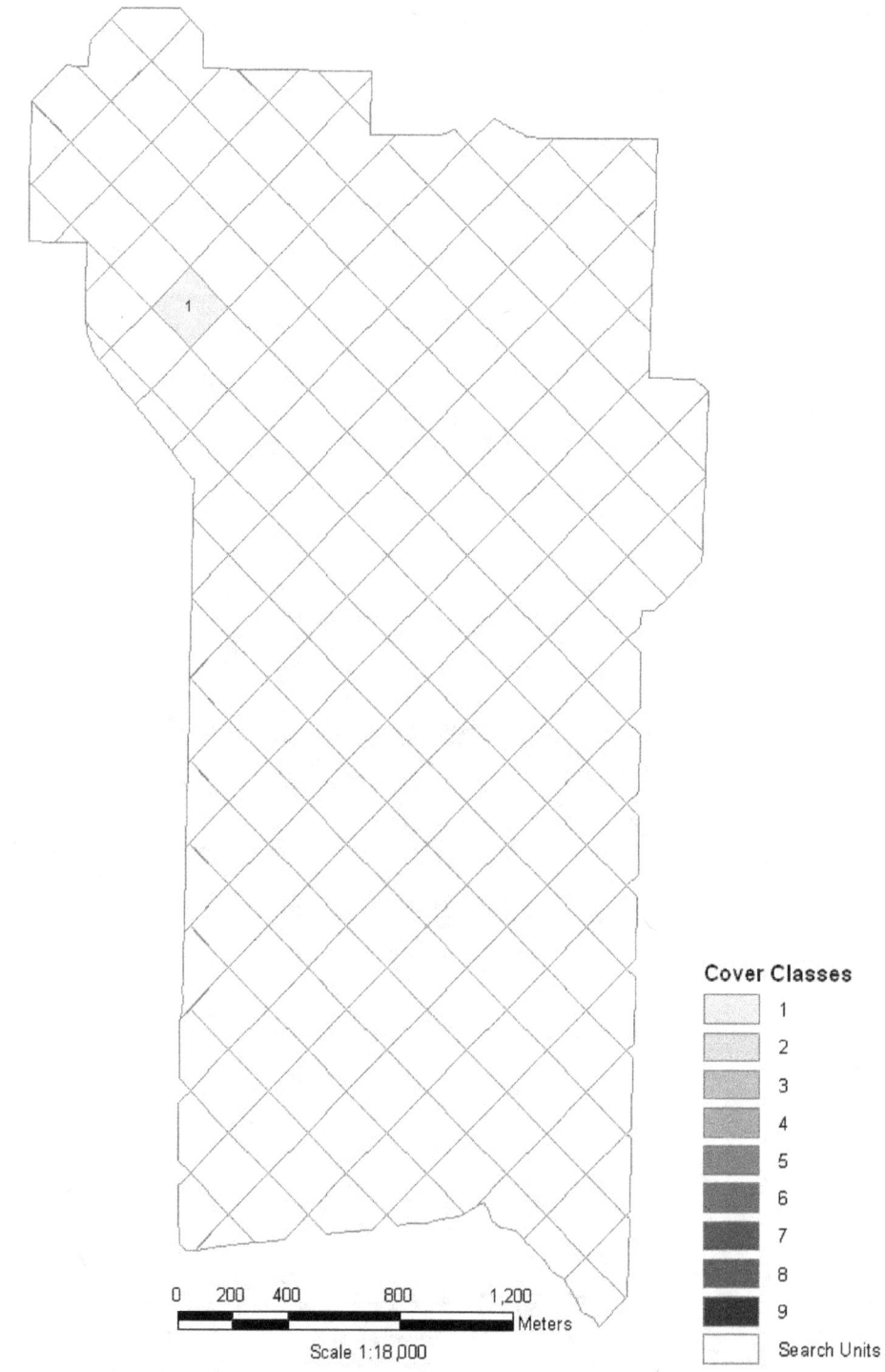

Figure 24. Abundance and distribution of *Miscanthus sinensis* (Chinese silvergrass) at Wilson's Creek National Battlefield, 2006. Cover classes are as follows: 1=0.1-0.9 m², 2=1-9.9 m², 3=10-49.9 m², 4= 50-99.9 m², 5=100-499.9 m², 6= 499.9-999.9 m², 7=1,000-4,999.9 m², 5,000-9,999.9 m², and 9=10,000-14,999.9. See figure 1 for areas not searched.

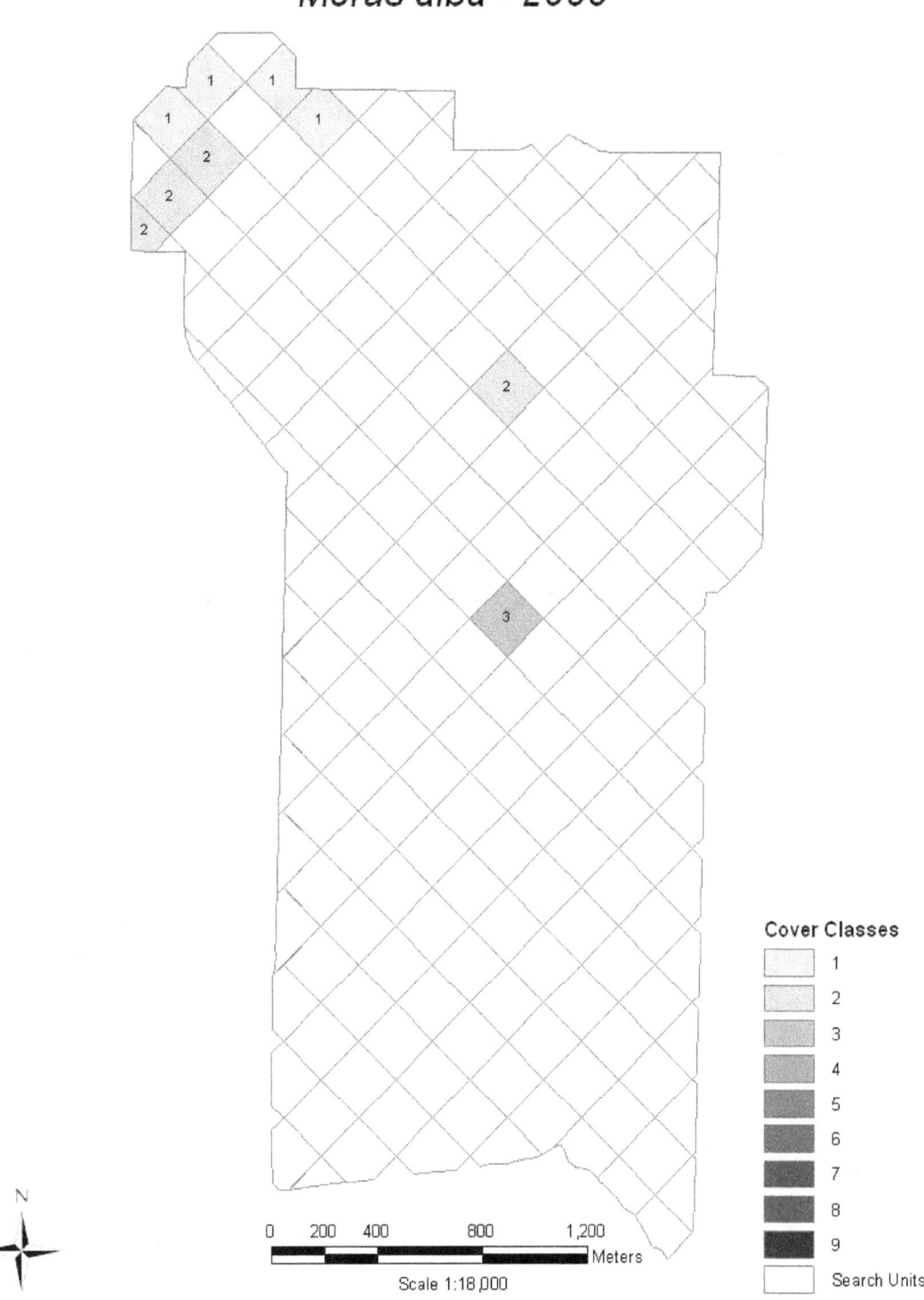

Morus alba - 2006

Cover Classes

1
2
3
4
5
6
7
8
9

Search Units

0   200   400   800   1,200
Meters
Scale 1:18,000

N

Figure 25. Abundance and distribution of *Morus aba* (white mulberry) at Wilson's Creek National Battlefield, 2006. Cover classes are as follows: 1=0.1-0.9 m^2, 2=1-9.9 m^2, 3=10-49.9 m^2, 4= 50-99.9 m^2, 5=100-499.9 m^2, 6= 499.9-999.9 m^2, 7=1,000-4,999.9 m^2, 5,000-9,999.9 m^2, and 9=10,000-14,999.9. See figure 1 for areas not searched.

Poa compressa - 2006

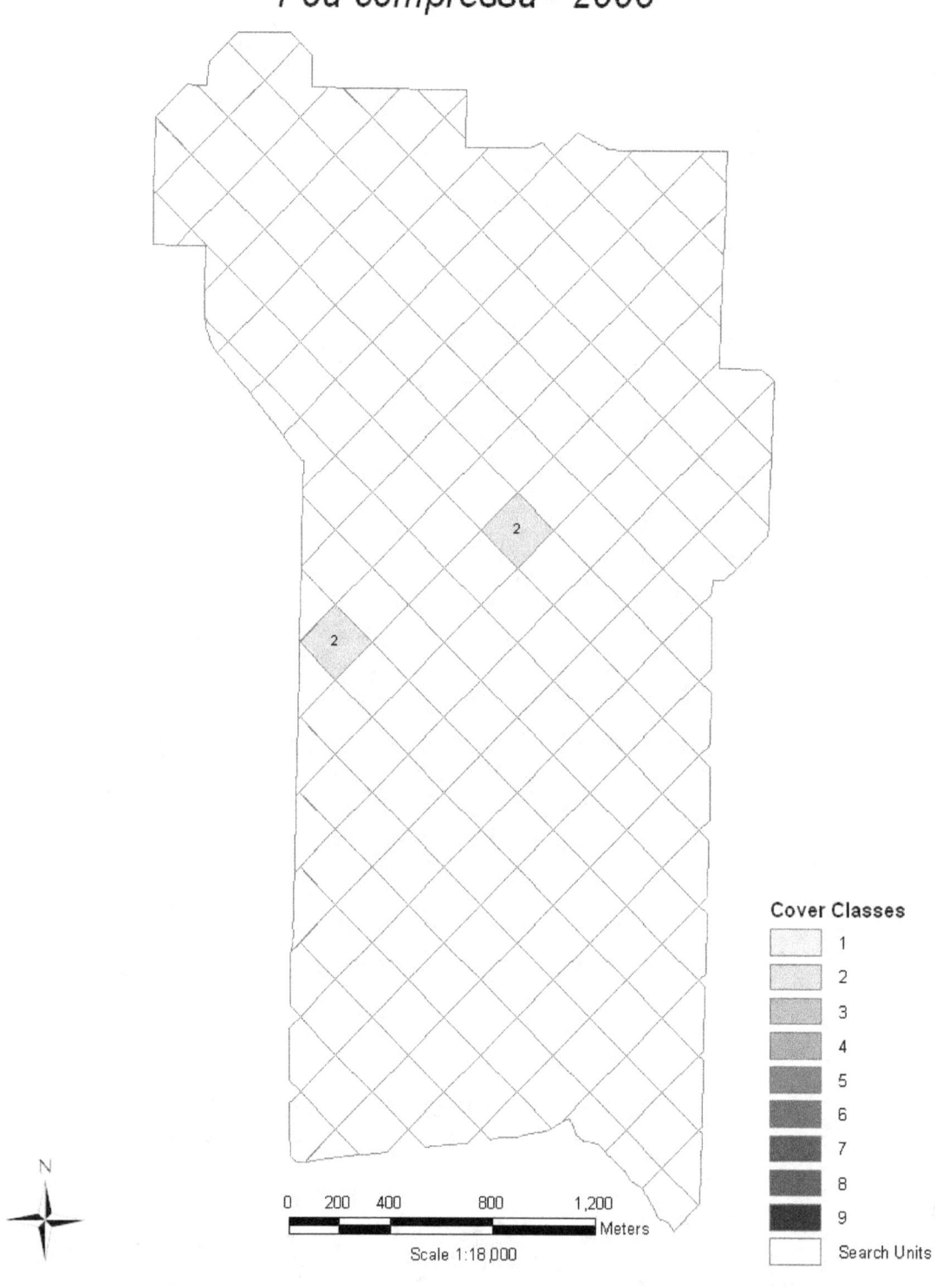

Figure 26. **Abundance and distribution of *Poa compressa* (Canada bluegrass) at Wilson's Creek National Battlefield, 2006. Cover classes are as follows: 1=0.1-0.9 m², 2=1-9.9 m², 3=10-49.9 m², 4= 50-99.9 m², 5=100-499.9 m², 6= 499.9-999.9 m², 7=1,000-4,999.9 m², 5,000-9,999.9 m², and 9=10,000-14,999.9. See figure 1 for areas not searched.**

Figure 27. Abundance and distribution of *Poa* spp. (bluegrass) at Wilson's Creek National Battlefield, 2006. Cover classes are as follows: 1=0.1-0.9 m², 2=1-9.9 m², 3=10-49.9 m², 4= 50-99.9 m², 5=100-499.9 m², 6= 499.9-999.9 m², 7=1,000-4,999.9 m², 5,000-9,999.9 m², and 9=10,000-14,999.9. See figure 1 for areas not searched.

Potentilla recta - 2006

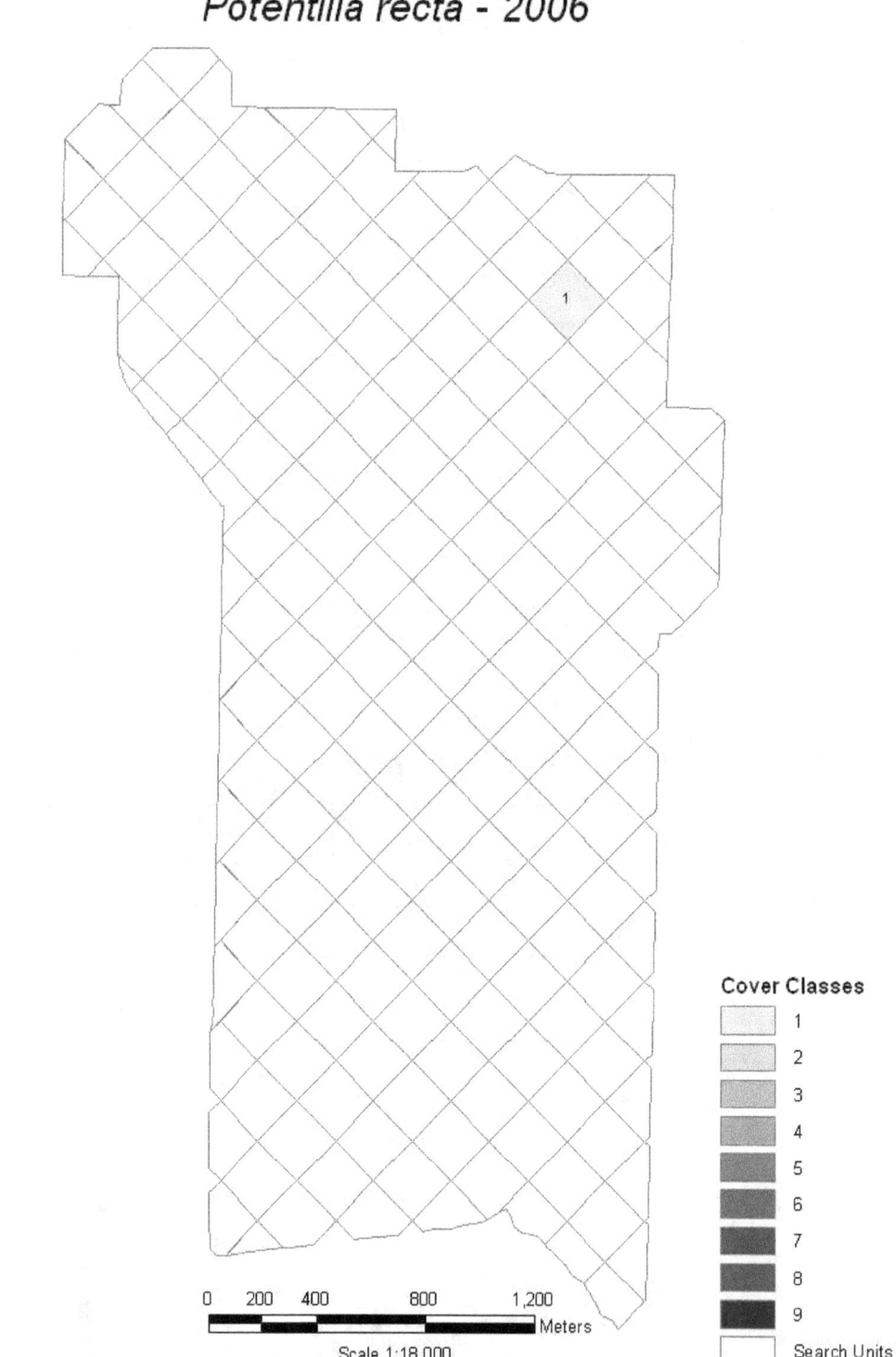

Cover Classes

1
2
3
4
5
6
7
8
9

Search Units

Scale 1:18,000

0   200   400   800   1,200
Meters

N

Figure 28. Abundance and distribution of *Potentilla recta* (sulphur cinquefoil) at Wilson's Creek National Battlefield, 2006. Cover classes are as follows: 1=0.1-0.9 m^2, 2=1-9.9 m^2, 3=10-49.9 m^2, 4= 50-99.9 m^2, 5=100-499.9 m^2, 6= 499.9-999.9 m^2, 7=1,000-4,999.9 m^2, 5,000-9,999.9 m^2, and 9=10,000-14,999.9. See figure 1 for areas not searched.

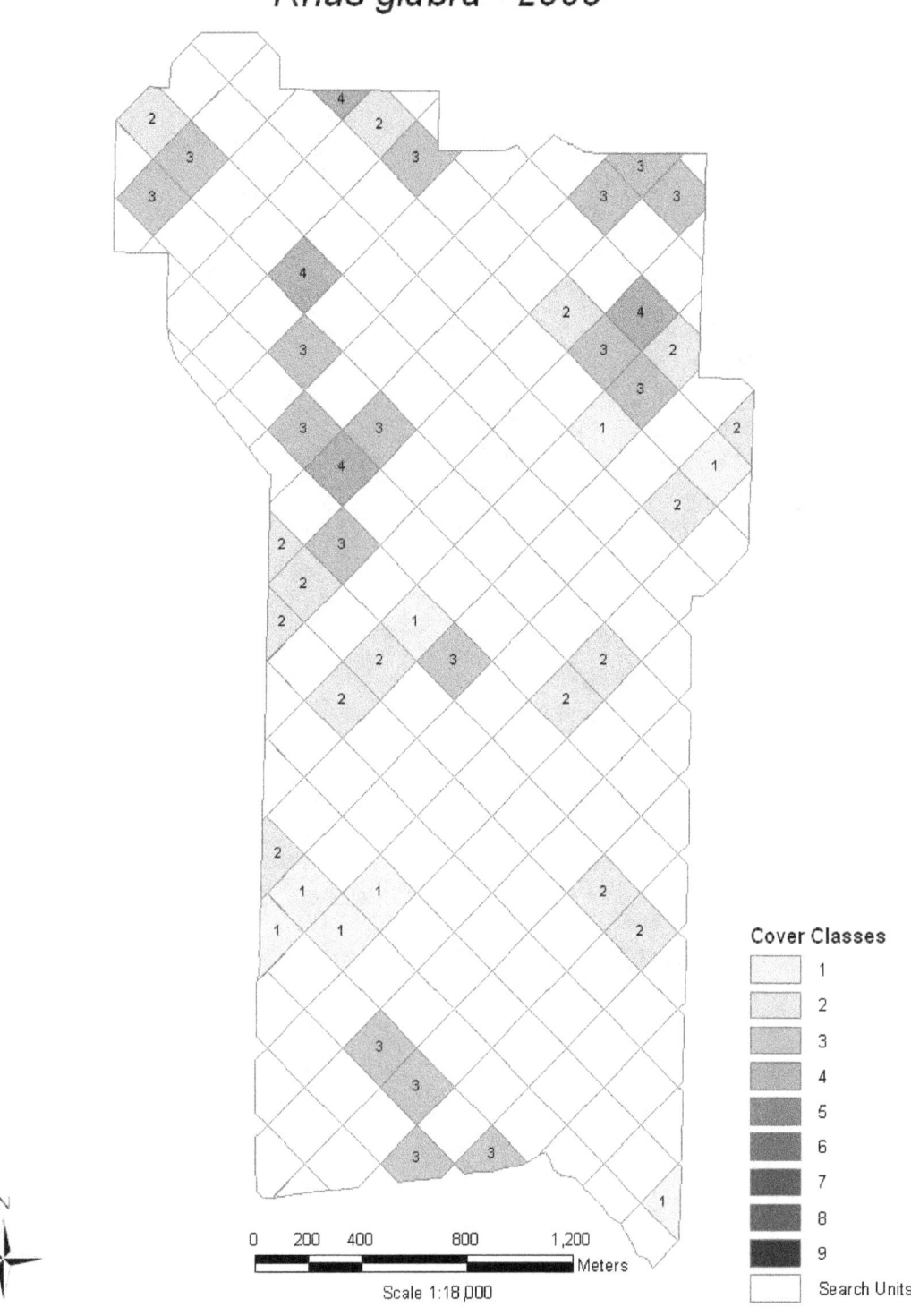

Figure 29. Abundance and distribution of *Rhus glabra* (smooth sumac) at Wilson's Creek National Battlefield, 2006. Cover classes are as follows: 1=0.1-0.9 m^2, 2=1-9.9 m^2, 3=10-49.9 m^2, 4= 50-99.9 m^2, 5=100-499.9 m^2, 6= 499.9-999.9 m^2, 7=1,000-4,999.9 m^2, 5,000-9,999.9 m^2, and 9=10,000-14,999.9. See figure 1 for areas not searched.

Figure 30. Abundance and distribution of *Rosa multiflora* (multiflora rose) at Wilson's Creek National Battlefield, 2006. Cover classes are as follows: 1=0.1-0.9 m², 2=1-9.9 m², 3=10-49.9 m², 4= 50-99.9 m², 5=100-499.9 m², 6= 499.9-999.9 m², 7=1,000-4,999.9 m², 5,000-9,999.9 m², and 9=10,000-14,999.9. See figure 1 for areas not searched.

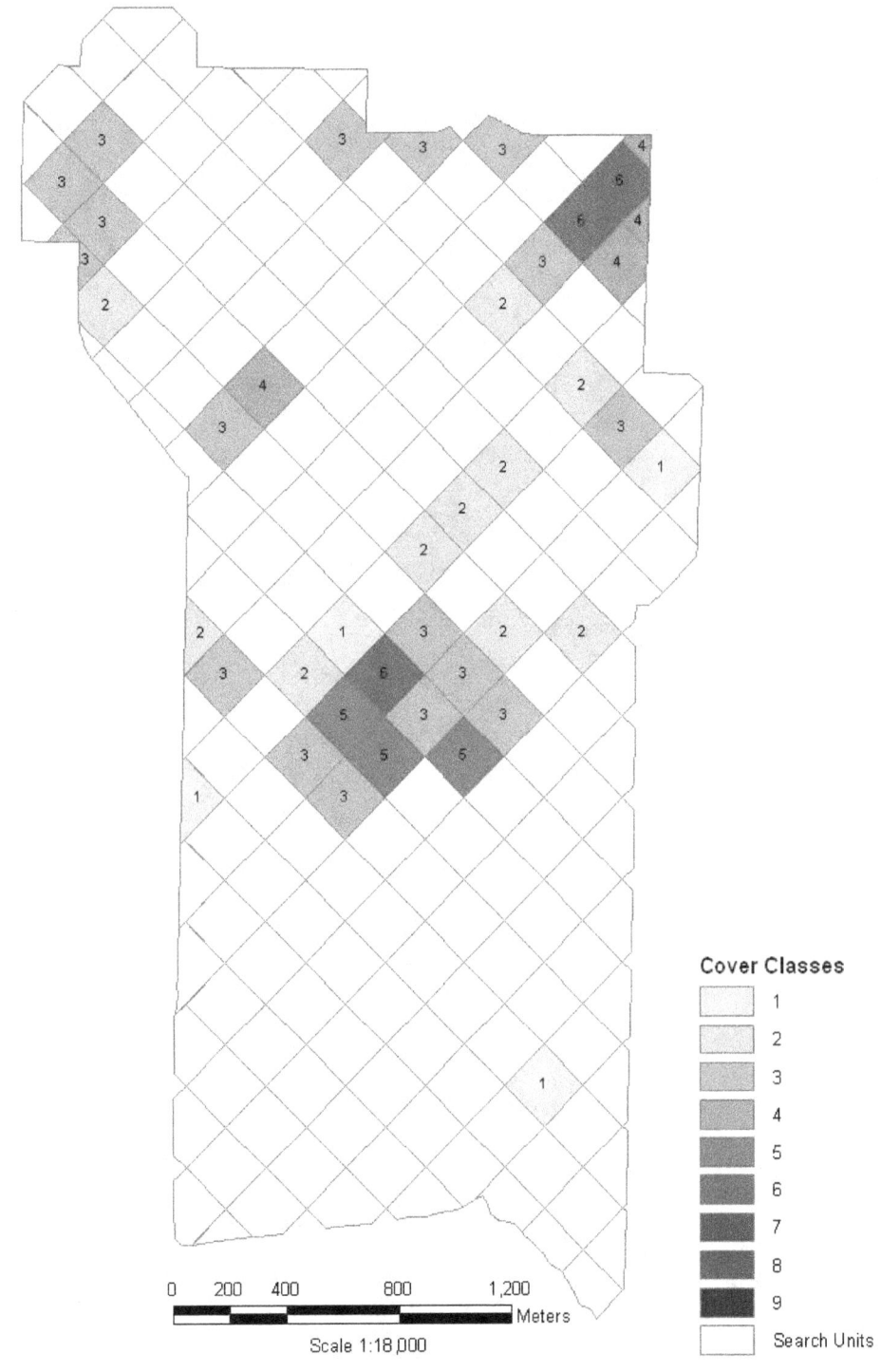

Figure 31. Abundance and distribution of *Schedonorus* spp. (fescue) at Wilson's Creek National Battlefield, 2006. Cover classes are as follows: 1=0.1-0.9 m², 2=1-9.9 m², 3=10-49.9 m², 4= 50-99.9 m², 5=100-499.9 m², 6= 499.9-999.9 m², 7=1,000-4,999.9 m², 5,000-9,999.9 m², and 9=10,000-14,999.9. See figure 1 for areas not searched.

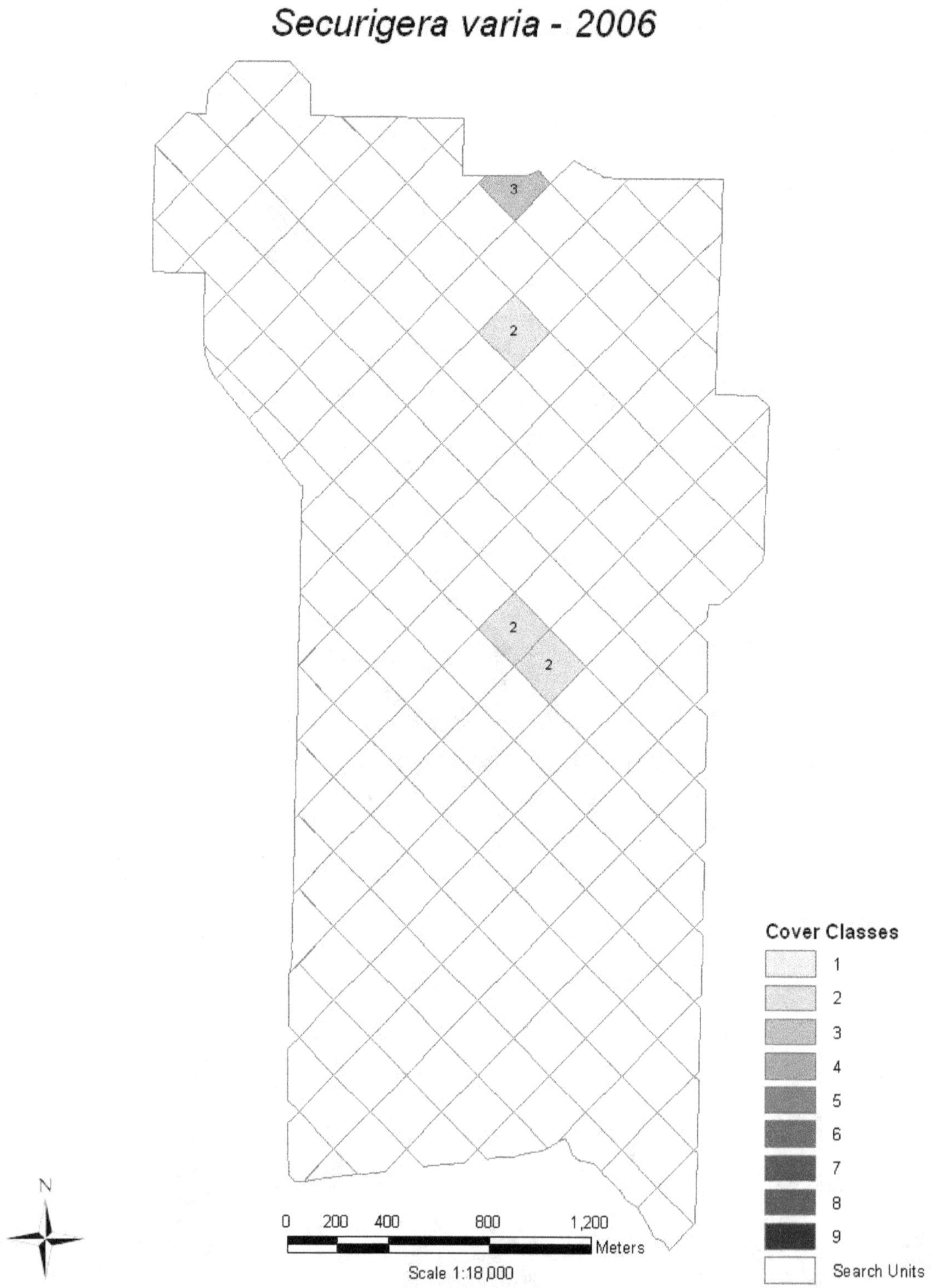

Figure 32. Abundance and distribution of *Securigera varia* (crown vetch) at Wilson's Creek National Battlefield, 2006. Cover classes are as follows: 1=0.1-0.9 m², 2=1-9.9 m², 3=10-49.9 m², 4= 50-99.9 m², 5=100-499.9 m², 6= 499.9-999.9 m², 7=1,000-4,999.9 m², 5,000-9,999.9 m², and 9=10,000-14,999.9. See figure 1 for areas not searched.

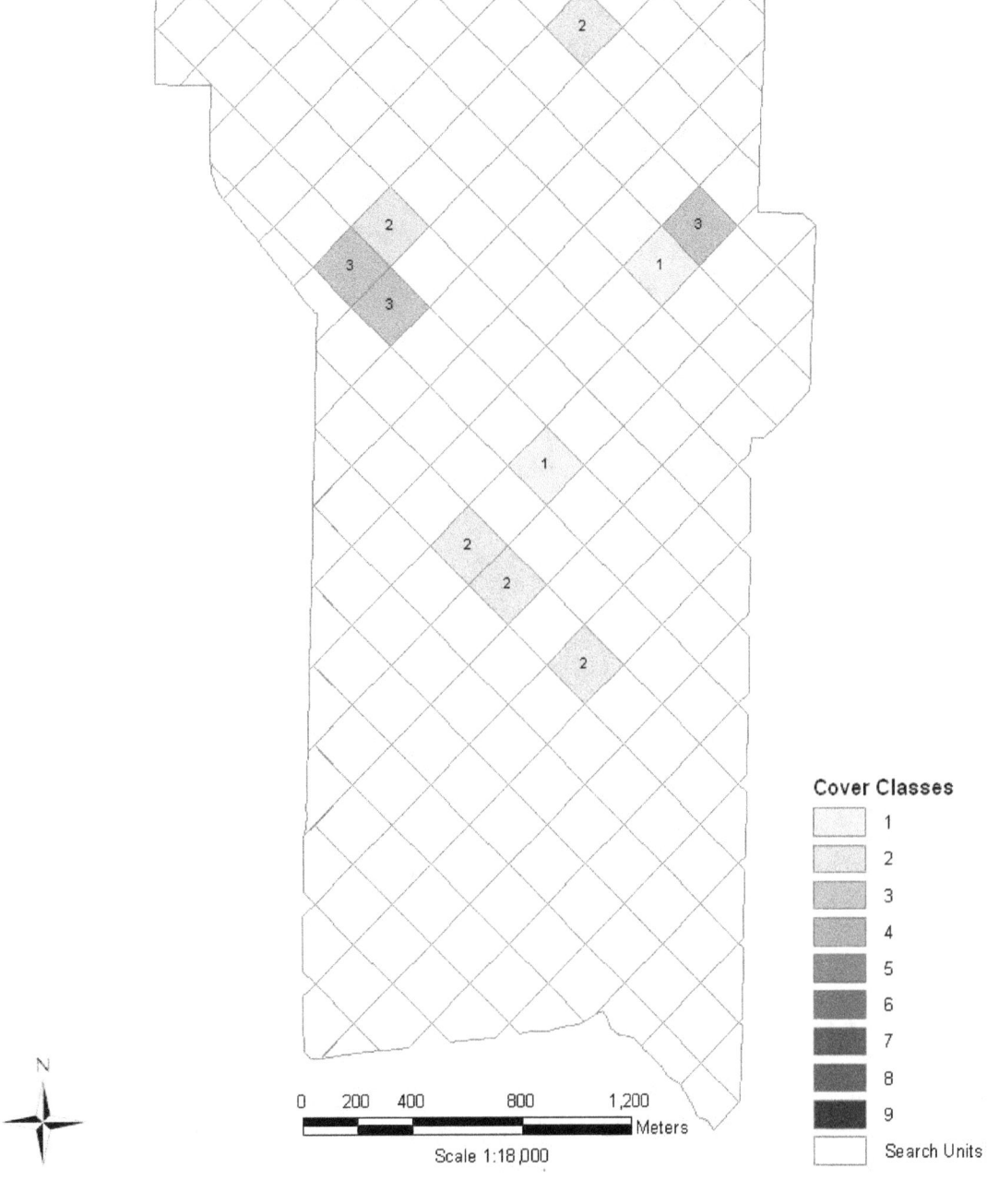

Sorghum halepense - 2006

Cover Classes

1
2
3
4
5
6
7
8
9
Search Units

Scale 1:18,000

Figure 33. Abundance and distribution of *Sorghum halepense* (Johnsongrass) at Wilson's Creek National Battlefield, 2006. Cover classes are as follows: 1=0.1-0.9 m^2, 2=1-9.9 m^2, 3=10-49.9 m^2, 4= 50-99.9 m^2, 5=100-499.9 m^2, 6= 499.9-999.9 m^2, 7=1,000-4,999.9 m^2, 5,000-9,999.9 m^2, and 9=10,000-14,999.9. See figure 1 for areas not searched.

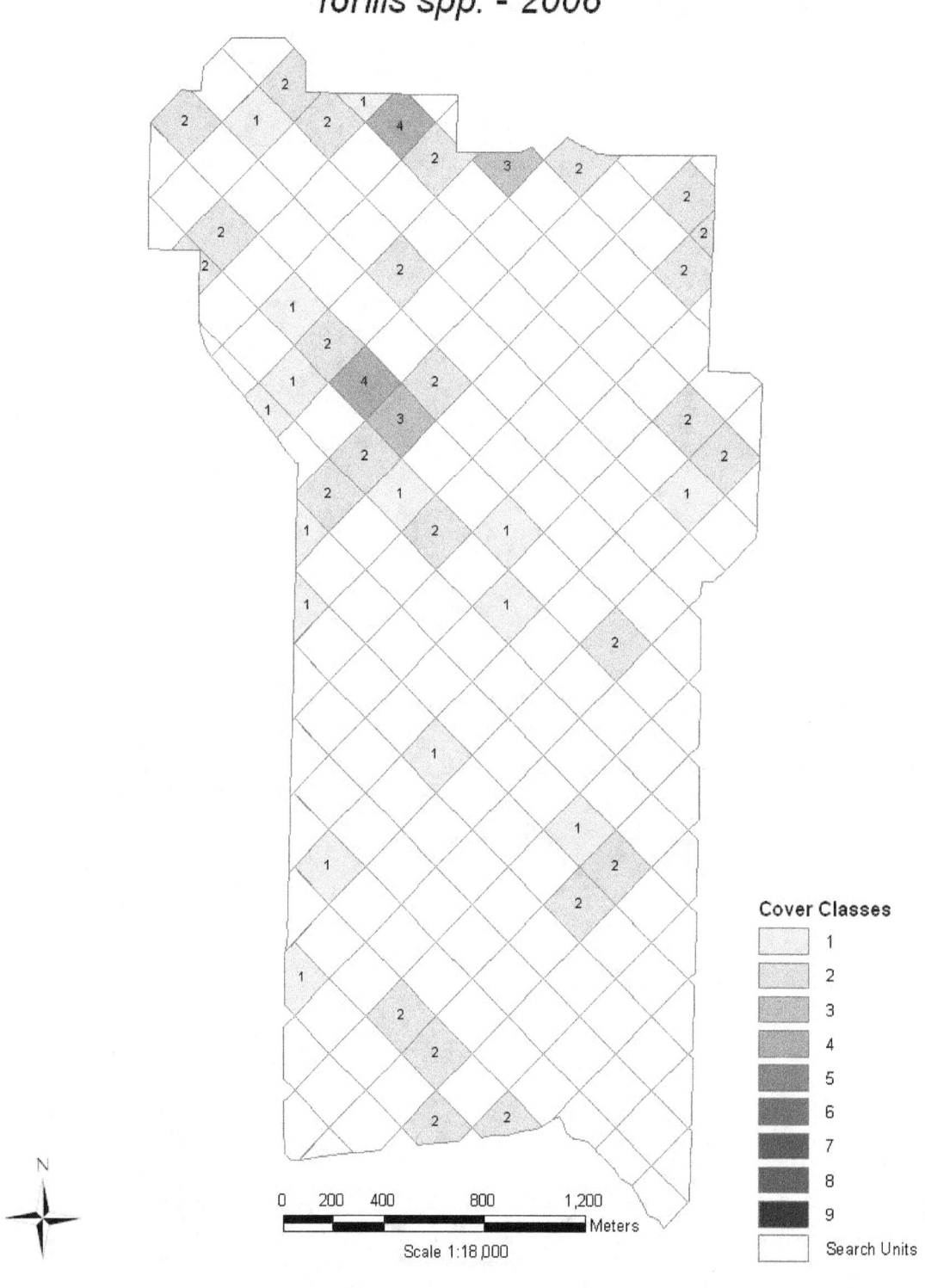

Figure 34. Abundance and distribution of *Torilis* spp. (hedgeparsley) at Wilson's Creek National Battlefield, 2006. Cover classes are as follows: 1=0.1-0.9 m², 2=1-9.9 m², 3=10-49.9 m², 4= 50-99.9 m², 5=100-499.9 m², 6= 499.9-999.9 m², 7=1,000-4,999.9 m², 5,000-9,999.9 m², and 9=10,000-14,999.9. See figure 1 for areas not searched.

Verbascum thapsus - 2006

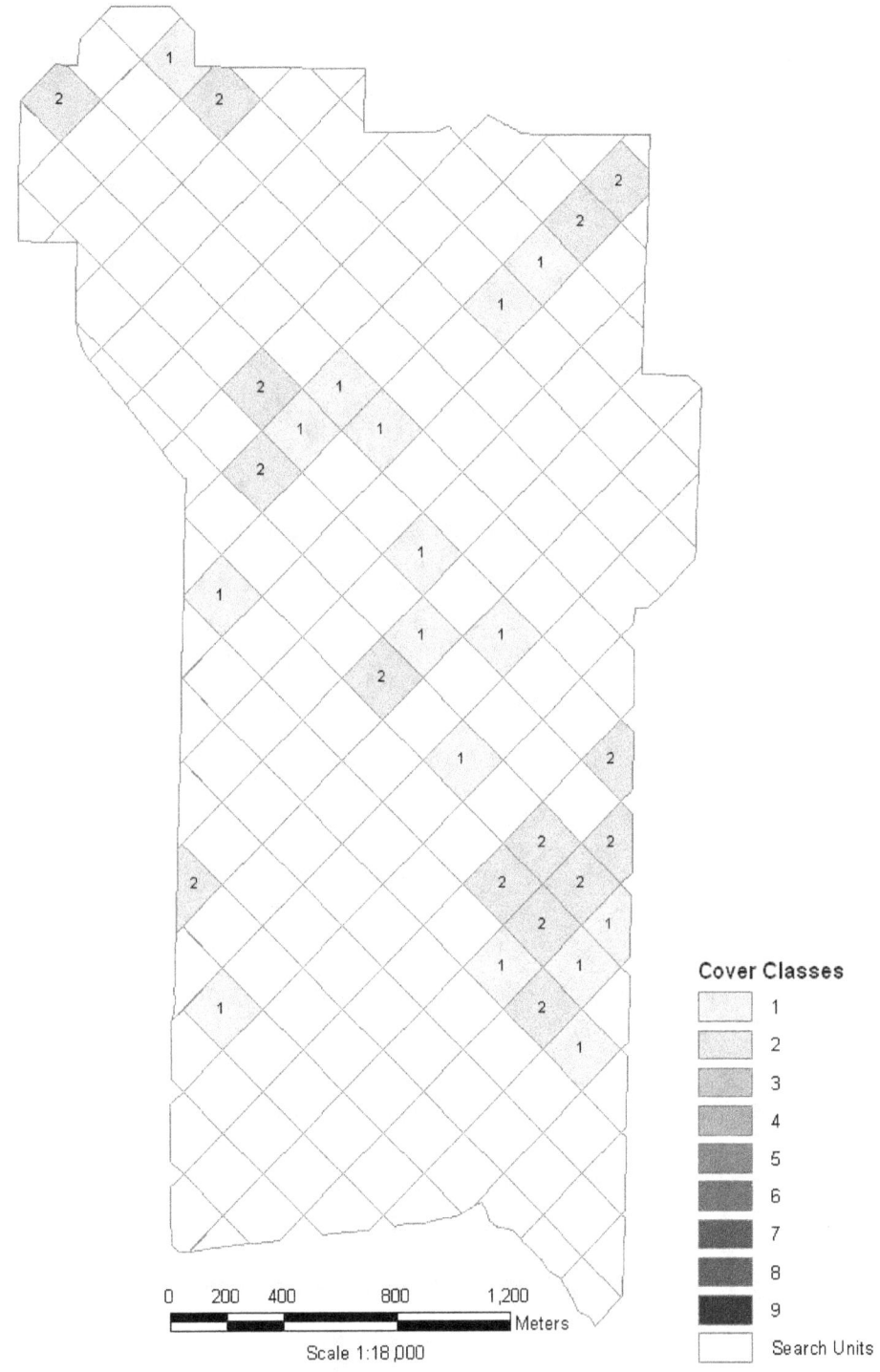

Figure 35. Abundance and distribution of *Verbascum thapsus* (common mullein) at Wilson's Creek National Battlefield, 2006. Cover classes are as follows: 1=0.1-0.9 m², 2=1-9.9 m², 3=10-49.9 m², 4= 50-99.9 m², 5=100-499.9 m², 6= 499.9-999.9 m², 7=1,000-4,999.9 m², 5,000-9,999.9 m², and 9=10,000-14,999.9. See figure 1 for areas not searched.

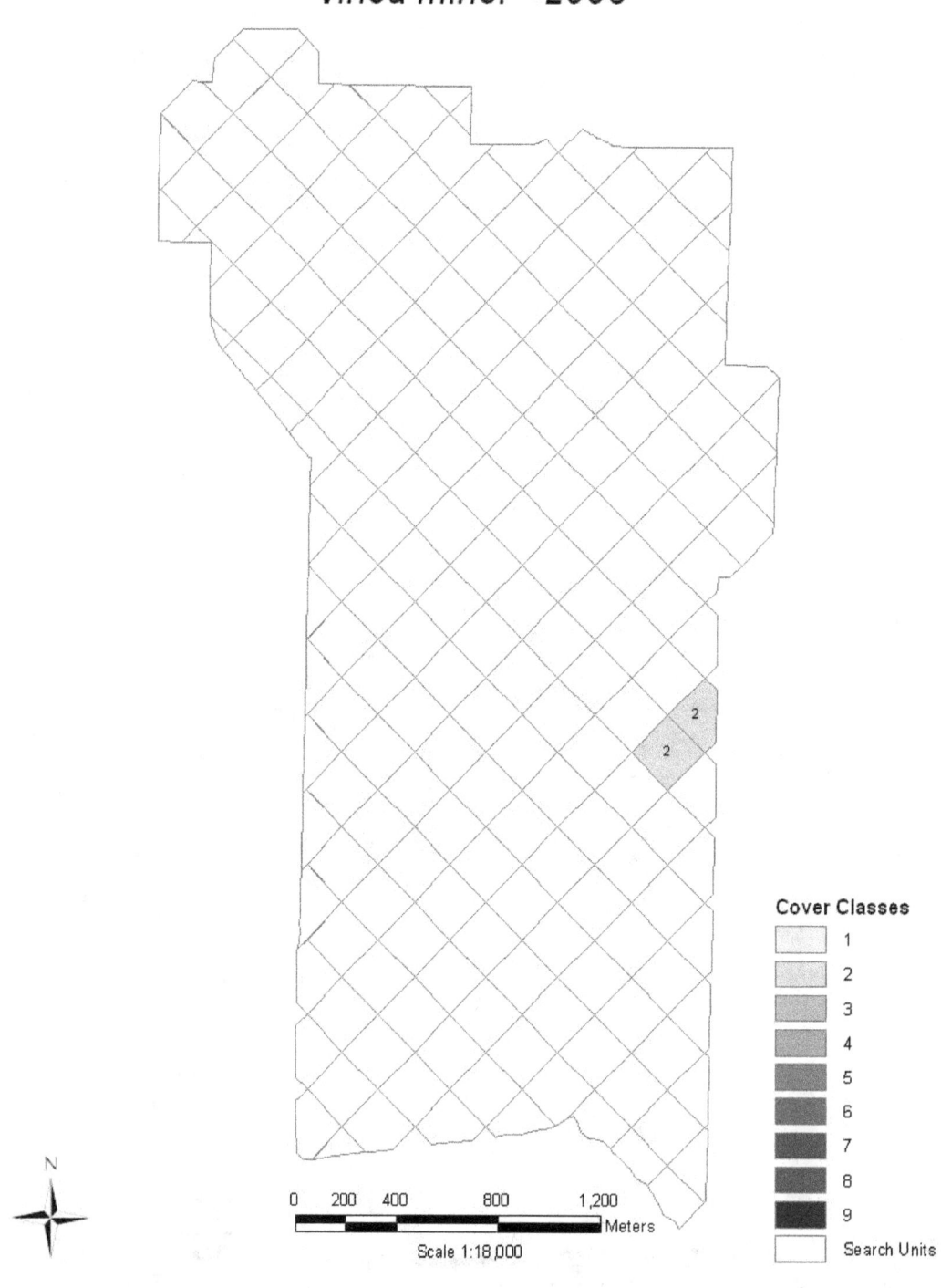

Figure 36. Abundance and distribution of *Vinca minor* (common periwinkle) at Wilson's Creek National Battlefield, 2006. Cover classes are as follows: 1=0.1-0.9 m², 2=1-9.9 m², 3=10-49.9 m², 4= 50-99.9 m², 5=100-499.9 m², 6= 499.9-999.9 m², 7=1,000-4,999.9 m², 5,000-9,999.9 m², and 9=10,000-14,999.9. See figure 1 for areas not searched.

The NPS has organized its parks with significant natural resources into 32 networks linked by geography and shared natural resource characteristics. HTLN is composed of 15 National Park Service (NPS) units in eight Midwestern states. These parks contain a wide variety of natural and cultural resources including sites focused on commemorating civil war battlefields, Native American heritage, westward expansion, and our U.S. Presidents. The Network is charged with creating inventories of its species and natural features as well as monitoring trends and issues in order to make sound management decisions. Critical inventories help park managers understand the natural resources in their care while monitoring programs help them understand meaningful change in natural systems and to respond accordingly. The Heartland Network helps to link natural and cultural resources by protecting the habitat of our history.

The I&M program bridges the gap between science and management with a third of its efforts aimed at making information accessible. Each network of parks, such as Heartland, has its own multi-disciplinary team of scientists, support personnel, and seasonal field technicians whose system of online databases and reports make information and research results available to all. Greater efficiency is achieved through shared staff and funding as these core groups of professionals augment work done by individual park staff. Through this type of integration and partnership, network parks are able to accomplish more than a single park could on its own.

The mission of the Heartland Network is to collaboratively develop and conduct scientifically credible inventories and long-term monitoring of park "vital signs" and to distribute this information for use by park staff, partners, and the public, thus enhancing understanding which leads to sound decision making in the preservation of natural resources and cultural history held in trust by the National Park Service.

www.nature.nps.gov/im/units/htln/

NPS D-76, March 2007